McGrews
1989

The Pilgrim Route to Santiago

The Pilgrim Route to Santiago

BRIAN & MARCUS TATE
Photographed by Pablo Keller

PHAIDON · OXFORD

Phaidon Press Limited, Littlegate House, St Ebbe's Street, Oxford OX1 1SQ

First published 1987

© Phaidon Press Limited 1987

Photographs © Pablo Keller 1987

British Library Cataloguing in Publication Data

Tate, Brian
    The pilgrim route to Santiago.
    1. Christian pilgrims and pilgrimages—
Spain—Santiago de Compostela
    I. Title   II. Tate, Marcus
    248.4'63'094652   BX2321.S
    ISBN 0-7148-2425-9

Printed in Spain by Heraclio Fournier SA, Vitoria

(title page) *View of the Pyrenees from the road between Jaca and San Juan de la Peña. The network of pilgrim routes north of the Pyrenees fuses together into single strands to cross the mountain barrier. Somport (summum portum) is one of the main points of entry from the north. From here the road descends to Jaca, the first major fortified settlement and capital of the expanding kingdom of Aragon. Slightly south of this route, buried in another ridge of mountains, lies the ancient monastery of San Juan de la Peña, pantheon of the Aragonese kings.*

† CONTENTS †

1 *The Romanesque Church of Santa Cruz de Serós, just south of the pilgrim road along the River Aragón between Pamplona and Jaca. The nave is eleventh century, the belfry late twelfth.*

For Beth, Caroline & Jitka

2 *Detail of the statue of St James, from the Church of St Jacques du Haut Pas in Paris. Many pilgrims from England came to be blessed at this church at the start of their pilgrimage. The statue seen here was damaged in the French Revolution.*

Introduction · The Mystery of St James

The sharp-eyed tourist travelling in south-west France and northern Spain may have spotted recently daubs of paint on roads and trees – parallel strokes of red and white in France, yellow in Spain – and casually wondered what they were. These signs are the work of various voluntary associations of the Confraternities of St James, and they mark out the ancient routes of the medieval pilgrimage through France to the shrine of St James the Great in the Cathedral of Compostela in distant north-west Spain. These routes thronged with pilgrims in the eleventh and twelfth centuries, and are still followed today by many travellers, single or in groups, who trek along the modern roads or ancient ways, on foot, on horseback, in cars, buses and caravans, visiting the shrines of saints or what remains of old hostels, hospitals, churches and monasteries, and reliving the experience of past centuries.

The medieval pilgrimage was a spiritual adventure which broke the routine of normal life. It was also the direct ancestor of the modern cultural tour that today encourages the traveller not only to wonder at the human achievements of past ages but also to consider the force which compelled thousands to abandon their ordinary lives and set forth across seas, rivers, mountain passes, pasture lands and unending plains in order to reach a remote church in Galicia.

Pilgrims were, and still are today, inspired by many motives – some not wholly religious. They came from a wide variety of backgrounds and along the road they founded churches, monasteries and hospitals; they robbed and killed, composed stories, legends, poems and songs, and slept rough in the hostels provided for them. The road became a cultural highway whose fragments can still be pieced together, either in the centre of noisy cities or in forgotten regions which modern roads have bypassed.

The traveller of today can re-create for himself the world of the pilgrim. If he has followed the route with any consistency, and can provide evidence of having visited the principal shrines along it, he too can apply in the Cathedral Secretariat of Santiago de Compostela for his Certificate of Pilgrimage or *compostelana* (Fig. 3), and eat his free meals in the kitchens of the Hospital of the Catholic Kings or *Hostal de los Reyes Católicos*, now a famous parador, under the towering granite façade of the cathedral.

3 *The modern equivalent of the medieval* compostelana, *a certificate which the pilgrim receives on completion of his pilgrimage. This may entitle him to hospitality at the Hostal de los Reyes Católicos, constructed in the fifteenth century by Fernando and Isabel. But in practice this depends on the season and the pressure of tourists.*

4 *Sixteenth-century plaster bas-relief of St James the Moorslayer, from the church of St James, beside the Renaissance monastery of the Knights of St James, the celebrated military order, in Leon. This work commemorates the saint's dramatic plunge from the sky at the Battle of Clavijo, when the Christian host was on the point of being overwhelmed by the Moors. This is a common theme of Jacobean iconography in Spain.*

How could it possibly have come about that the legend of an apostle martyred in the Middle East was linked with an obscure hamlet in the most remote and primitive region of early medieval Spain; and that from this strange combination emerged one of the most popular manifestations of spirituality in medieval Europe?

Since the apogee of the pilgrimage in the Middle Ages many people, and not only Spaniards, believed on the basis of certain medieval sources a number of basic things about St James the Great. They affirmed that he had preached in the Iberian Peninsula, and that during his stay the Virgin Mary had appeared to him on the banks of the River Ebro. St James had then returned to Jerusalem where, in AD 42, he became the first apostle to be martyred for his faith. His body was taken to Spain and buried at a spot upon which was built the Cathedral of Santiago de Compostela. His divine powers not only protected the pilgrims who came to worship at his shrine but also enabled a tiny Christian army to massacre thousands of infidels at the Battle of Clavijo in AD 859. For this action he was chosen as the patron saint of Spain.

5 *Legend dating back to the ninth century recalls that the body and severed head of the martyr St James were transported in a stone boat from the Holy Land to the far reaches of the Atlantic shores of north-west Spain. Local tradition has it that the point of landing was Padrón, a small fishing village in Galicia, whose name means 'stone marker'. This eighteenth-century fountain and shrine in the village of Padrón depicts the legend.*

This is the Santiago 'creed' and it has, in part or in whole, survived controversy and competition. However, controversy and competition there has always been from different quarters and for different reasons: the exaltation of other divine powers, the claims of other churches and their shrines, the refusal of landowners and institutions to pay a general tithe to sustain the canons of the cathedral on the authority of documents and charters that were, in the eyes of some, demonstrably false.

At the centre of the 'creed' lies the necessary belief that St James's whole body was contained in the shrine at Santiago. Around this central belief, like an elaborate altar over a relic, there accumulated a series of legends which articulated that belief and added to the martyr a number of other guises: the pilgrim, the giver of absolution, the curer of physical and mental illness, the *Santiago Matamoros* or Moor-slayer (Fig. 4). It is a many-faceted figure fashioned to reflect the aspirations of quite different sets of people in different places. Episodes of his apostolate, his miraculous translation, and examples of his curative powers can be found in reliefs, frescos, paintings and stained-glass all over Western Europe. These secondary legends were given power by major artists and craftsmen and go a long way to explain the reverence in which he was held in such diverse places, almost equalling that of the first-rank figures of Mark, John, Paul, Peter and the Virgin Mary.

The present book aims above all to evoke through prose and photographic image the visual experience of the journey to the shrine of St James, alternating between the works of the creative imagination in stone, brick, glass and paint and the infinite variety of landscapes in which they are set. It also places the emphasis more firmly on Spain than on France, because this is the less well-known part of the route.

The opening chapter deals in generalities: the phenomenon of pilgrimage, the motives of the pilgrim, the pursuit of spiritual and bodily renewal, the nature and importance of relics, the character of the pilgrimage church and concludes with a description of the principal routes through France to the Pyrenees en route to the shrine. The subsequent chapters take up the main route across the Pyrenees and northern Spain, ending up in Padrón, originally a fishing village on an estuary leading to the Atlantic (Fig. 5). There one can still see on request, under the altar of the parish church, the ancient stone post to which, it is alleged, the boat was moored which brought the body of St James to Spain seven days after he was beheaded in Jerusalem.

English forms of foreign names are used in all cases where they are current, for example, Cordoba, Leon, Aragon (referring to towns or principalities). Otherwise the foreign form is used, such as the River Aragón, San Juan de Ortega, Santo Domingo de la Calzada. The names Santiago and Compostela (Latin: Compostella) refer to Santiago de Compostela. We hope we shall be excused for referring to the pilgrim as 'he'. There were notable women pilgrims, such as Marjory Kempe from King's Lynn, but many fewer than there were men.

I † The Pilgrim and the Medieval Roads through France

In the mid-thirteenth century a clerk named Gonzalo put into verse a collection of miracles said to have been worked by the Virgin Mary. Gonzalo lived in the Spanish Monastery of San Millán de la Cogolla set in a clearing near the hamlet of Berceo in the Rioja, the contested border country between the provinces of Castile and Navarre. The main characteristic of Gonzalo's anthology was that it was written in the common tongue of the region, in Castilian, and was intended not only for the local population but also for those who were travelling the road which led from the Pyrenees to the great shrine of Santiago de Compostela in Galicia in the north-western corner of Spain. It is also amongst the first poems in Castilian that can be attributed to a named poet, and is of interest both as an expression of, and insight into, popular sentiment of that time. The poet names himself in the second quatrain and the opening stanzas can be translated thus:

Friends and subjects of the all-powerful Lord,
If you would grant me the favour of listening to my words,
I'd like to tell you of a strange event,
Which in the end you'll accept as the truth.

I, master Gonzalo, from the village of Berceo,
While on pilgrimage chanced upon a meadow,
Green, untrodden, full of flowers,
Just the resting-place for an exhausted traveller.[1]

This meadow, we discover subsequently, is not an ordinary one, but a magic place, an earthly paradise where his tired body is restored. Then he explains, in simple terms, the deeper meaning of his parable:

All of us who can use our feet and legs,
Those who are shut in prison, or lie upon their beds,
We are, all of us, pilgrims set upon the roads.
St Peter has said as much, and he is our witness.

Gonzalo has focused the attention of his audience on an activity in which most of them were engaged – the pilgrimage – comparing it with an exciting adventure, and then extending the experience to encompass all Christians. These pilgrims, either visiting the shrine of

6,7 *Thirteenth-century stained glass, Cathedral of Notre Dame, Chartres. These details are from the Charlemagne window, one of a pair of windows in the choir. One window is dedicated to Charlemagne and the Song of Roland, the other to the life of St James the Great. The Charlemagne window was paid for by the Fur Merchants Guild. In a detail* (above), *Charlemagne appears in full armour of the year 1200. Another part of the window* (right) *shows the armies of Charlemagne and the Moors meeting head-on in a cavalry charge. The Franks have pointed shields; the infidels have round ones. After the battle Charlemagne returns to France and a subsequent scene (not illustrated) shows St James appearing to him in a dream and pleading with him to return to Spain.*

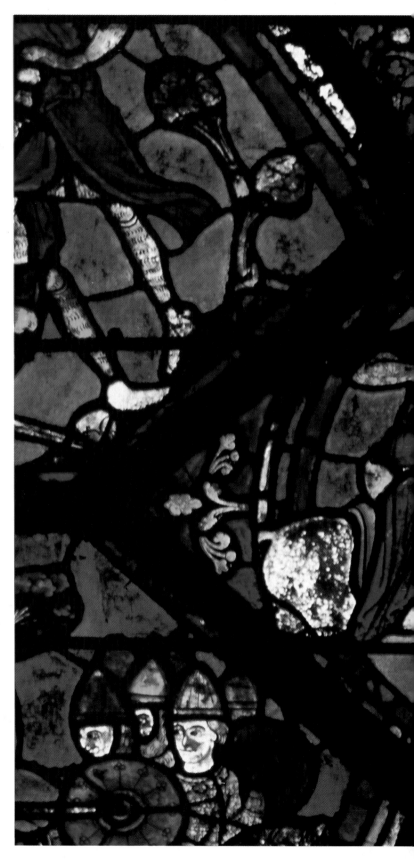

San Millán, or combining it with the journey to Compostela, represented a significant proportion of the population of Central and Western Europe from the eleventh through to the fifteenth century.

Evidence shows that the pilgrimage was not an activity that persisted with the same vitality throughout all the ages of Christendom, so that there must have been other circumstances to encourage the enterprise during this period. As for motive, none of the modern writers can agree upon a single impulse. It would seem that motives might have ranged from the purest longing for spiritual rebirth to the most secular of inducements: adventure, excitement, reprieve from punishment by the law or cure of bodily ills. Such incitements prevailed in the past and have endured, continuing to inspire today, although the activity is no longer as central to Christian faith as it was; nor has it the force in the West which it exercises in Islamic countries where pilgrimage is one of the commandments of truly religious life.

The phrase of St Peter alluded to in the above poem contains the notion that we are all pilgrims whilst on earth, and this has manifested itself in various ways throughout the history of Christianity. The notion, or myth, of the pilgrim's journey also provides a particularly useful mirror in which medieval attitudes to, and perceptions of, early Christian history are reflected – both literally and metaphorically. Early ascetic movements in the Western Church can be seen to demonstrate an impulse to withdraw from an alien and threatening world, and to endure a temporary state until Paradise in the next world is attained. The wanderings of the early holy men foreshadowed the formation of reclusive, isolated monastic communities and, later, mass movements on the road. Both the monk and the pilgrim withdraw from the routines of secular life, but the pilgrim is following a literal path which he hopes will lighten his burden of sin.

It is significant that the portals of the west fronts of cathedral, church and abbey reiterate the incessant and relentless battle between the Devil and Christ for the possession of the human soul. This reflects an acute consciousness within medieval society of the physical presence of evil, the concept of demoniacal possession and the intervention of malignant forces in the form of fire, flood, famine or plague which persuades the Christian to seek protection by calling on other supernatural sources as the only impregnable defence against eternal damnation. Survival and salvation was not secure for everyone; it was the result of an intervention close to the miraculous which, if it did not come direct from God, was effected through the mediation of saintly figures and martyrs who exerted to the full their powers in the places where their bodies or their relics lay.

As imagination was so susceptible to the presence of evil, so strong and immediate in its impact on mind and body, it was correspondingly sensitive to the presence of countervailing powers emanating from those sites hallowed by the bodies of the saints. It was held that a shrine was a particular point of intersection of the secular and spiritual where the potential of the suppliant's faith would be assisted

8 *Apse and crossing tower of the twelfth-century Church of St Pierre, Parthenay le Vieux. The so-called Pilgrim's Guide,* Liber Sancti Jacobi, *is attributed to Aimery Picaud, who was born in this village. On the façade of the church are the remains of a stone bas-relief of a mounted equestrian figure. The figure appears elsewhere on the pilgrim route: in Melle (Fig. 37) and in the porch of Santa María, Carrión de los Condes.*

to call forth the powers of the deity. It was a special place where the efficacy of prayer could be enhanced beyond measure.

If Christ had performed miracles, and if he had promised that his apostles would perform works to match those he had performed himself, it is not surprising that the figure of St James the Great, an apostle close to Christ and the first to be martyred, should exert such a powerful attraction.

Most of the relics one encounters in the history of the early Church could be classed as objects closely associated with holy men and women. The period of the early persecutions which followed the Crucifixion was fundamental in promoting veneration for the relics of the martyrs; the chains they wore, for example, or the places where their bodies were buried. The 'tomb shrine' became a central focus of attention. As the places of burial were often unknown, spectacular discoveries were effected by dreams and visions which proliferated from the fifth century onwards and in many cases offered political advantages to their discoverers or their patrons, as can be seen later in the case of the body of St James.

As it became increasingly necessary to possess a relic for the consecration of a church, the demand led to the relaxation of, and

9 *Angel on interior corner of crossing tower, Abbey Church of Ste Foy, Conques. The archangel Gabriel and other important members of the celestial hierarchy are often set high up in medieval churches to watch over the fabric of the building.*

10 *Head of the reliquary statue of Ste Foy, Abbey Church of Ste Foy, Conques. The relics of the saint, an early Gallic martyr, are contained in the chest of this wooden statue, which is covered with gold and silver sheets and studded with precious stones.*

eventual disregard for, the customary rules about movement and dismemberment of bodies. Duplications, deceptions and thefts were perpetrated, even by figures who ultimately became saints themselves. There were debates about authenticity, but this usually meant an attack on someone else's apparently spurious relic and a defence of one's own.

The lives of these saints and the miracles performed by their relics were shaped into a special literary genre of hagiography and circulated throughout Europe in anthologies, while sculptural representations with appropriate and often novel symbols of the saints appeared in porches, cloisters and stained glass. The relics themselves were encased in precious metals often reflecting their form; the Cross, for example, the Nail, or parts of the bodies of the saints. Larger items were contained in chest-like tombs, or in seated or standing statues, all beautifully gilded or inlaid.

A famous medieval compilation makes clear what is demanded of the pilgrim, who it is that can benefit from pilgrimage, what one should know of St James's history and his powers, and what routes led to his shrine. The *Liber Sancti Jacobi* is the source to which all scholars still turn for information. This Latin manuscript is also known as the *Codex Calixtinus* because its authorship was falsely attributed to Pope Calixtus II (1119-24). It dates from between 1139 and 1165. There are about half-a-dozen manuscript copies preserved in Compostela, Paris, Rome, London, Ripoll and Alcobaça in Portugal. It embraces a remarkable range of material in its five books. The first contains a series of sermons and hymns, the second an anthology of miracles performed by St James and the third another collection of stories associated with his life and the discovery of his tomb. The fourth consists of a history, the *Historia Karoli Magni et Rotholandi*, attributed to the 'warrior' Bishop Turpin, which deals chiefly with the history of Compostela and the campaigns of the eighth-century Emperor Charlemagne. The fifth is a medieval Pilgrim's Guide which sketches out the French and Spanish routes, points out the chief shrines and offers advice to the traveller on all sorts of topics. All of this material, one is informed, was put into shape by a French cleric named Aimery Picaud of Parthenay le Vieux in about 1139, after he had made a pilgrimage on horseback, thus leaving to posterity a picturesque document which is full of asides on the habits and customs of peoples along the route.[2]

In Book One, an elaborate sermon sketched out what was to be demanded from the pilgrim. The *Veneranda Dies*, as it was named, was supposed to be read to pilgrims on the second feast-day of St James, 20 December (the main feast-day is 25 July). The author makes it plain that the journey to Santiago cannot itself save the sinner:

The way of St James is fine but narrow, as narrow as the path of salvation. That path is the shunning of vice, the mortification of the flesh, and the increasing of virtue...The pilgrim may bring with him no money at all, except

perhaps to distribute it to the poor on the road. Those who sell their property before leaving must give every penny of it to the poor, for if they spend it on their own journey they are departing from the path of God. In times past the faithful had but one heart and soul, and they held all property in common, owning nothing of their own; just so, the pilgrims of today must hold everything in common and travel together with one heart and soul...Goods shared in common are worth much more than goods owned by individuals. Thus it is that the pilgrim who dies on the road with money in his pocket is permanently excluded from the kingdom of heaven...If the Lord chose to enter Jerusalem on a mule rather than on a horse, then what are we to think of those who parade up and down before us on horseback?...If St Peter entered Rome with nothing but a crucifix, why do so many pilgrims come here with bulging purses and trunks of spare clothes, eating succulent food and drinking heady wine?...St James was a wanderer without money or shoes and yet ascended to heaven as soon as he died; what then will happen to those who make opulent progresses to his shrine surrounded by all the evidence of their wealth?[3]

11 *Pilgrim graffiti on the wall of the old hospital outside Pons. Where pilgrims rested they often left simple records of their passage, carved representations of horseshoes, crosses, crests and initials. One can also see such markings on the façade of the abbey church of Arthous in Lower Navarre. But many other traces have been destroyed as the buildings have been demolished for road widening.*

A few would obey these words to the letter, but churchmen did not want to discourage individuals from any social level. They appealed to the three estates within the medieval social hierarchy *bellatores* (knights), *oratores* (clergy), *laboratores* (peasantry), and wanted in particular to encourage the aristocracy to consider this path to salvation.

Book Four of the *Liber Sancti Jacobi* linked the traditional memories of the campaigns of Charlemagne against the Moors with the figure of the apostle. This particular book contained a famous chronicle attributed to the Bishop Turpin, who was supposed to have accompanied the Emperor in his famous invasion of Spain of the eighth century. This chronicle held that St James appeared to the Emperor in a vision and beseeched him to come to Spain and rescue it from the Moors. As a result St James would assure him celestial glory and eternal fame amongst men. The remainder of the narrative outlined the fabled deeds that spanned the pilgrim road, reaching an apocalyptic climax on the pass at Roncesvalles where Roland, Charlemagne's nephew, died defending the rear of his uncle's army after proudly refusing to blow his horn to summon reinforcements. But Charlemagne was to return in triumph and the relics of the great battles were distributed amongst sites that later became centres of pilgrimage, because the noble dead had become martyrs and were to receive, like the earlier persecuted saints, the cult of martyrdom.

The myth of Charlemagne, the pilgrim to St James, was thus cultivated to persuade the 'warrior' aristocracy not to disregard this way of salvation. In the eleventh century, William II, Count of Poitou and Duke of Aquitaine, is recorded as visiting Rome each year or, if that was not possible, then the shrine of St James, and 'such was the splendour of his retinue and the nobility of his learning that onlookers took him for a king rather than a duke'.[4] Arnau Mir of Tost in the eastern Pyrenees made his fortune as a mercenary for both Christian and Moslem in that century of opportunity, the eleventh, and went on a pilgrimage, a rich man, to Santiago in 1071.[5] Richard Mauleverer, a Yorkshire landowner, visited the shrine in the first years of the twelfth century. Ansgot of Burwell in Lincolnshire, the earliest pilgrim from England known to us by name, wanted to found in his home town a priory dependent on the great Benedictine Abbey of La Sauve Majeure, in return for the hospitality shown to him on return from Santiago at the end of the eleventh century.[6]

Apart from the *oratores* and the *bellatores*, the spiritual leaders of the eleventh and the twelfth centuries aimed at a truly popular audience and succeeded in massing great mobs of pilgrims who straggled along the roads to Spain. Their task was facilitated by a general fear that the world might end around the millennium or other critical dates, and this contributed to galvanize people into action.

Recent writers on the topic of pilgrimage and penance agree on two things; that from the late tenth to the twelfth century the practice of undertaking a pilgrimage to a known shrine became increasingly widespread, and that this expansion was related to the way in which

12 (opposite) *View of west front of Abbey Church of Ste Foy, Conques. This remarkable twelfth-century church contains the reliquary statue of Ste Foy (Fig. 10). The statue was deliberately stolen from the church of Agen by a monk of Ste Foy in about AD 865-6. Agen tried sporadically to retrieve the relic, but eventually had to accept this holy theft, or* furtum sacrum, *by which the relic had allowed itself to be 'liberated' and resettled elsewhere. These holy thefts were a characteristic phenomenon of the medieval trade in relics. Even the most famous churches, such as St Mark's in Venice, hold relics that were stolen deliberately from other sites.*

the Church dealt with the expiation of sin. The early Irish and Anglo-Saxon theologians made severe demands on the confessed sinner and laid down firmly a list of appropriate penances for sins. When such penance was completed, and not before, absolution was granted. Pilgrimage was often prescribed and, in grave cases, amounted to perpetual exile. This could mean that sinners remained unreconciled with the Church for long periods of time. From the end of the tenth century, a change gradually took place whereby the penitent was readmitted to Church after confession, but was still expected to take care of lightening the burden of his sins which otherwise remained with him only to be expiated in some purgatorial process. As one writer puts it, 'penance as "satisfaction" for sin came to receive greater emphasis than the older idea of penance as "spiritual medicine".'[7] So that while absolution came more quickly, the exercise of penance in public acts of pilgrimage became more frequent and prolonged, and was used also by the criminal courts. In the past the particular shrine to which the penitent was directed was not of any great importance; but later the penitential pilgrimage began to be connected with certain shrines and the belief grew that formal visits to these places could lead to remission of sins. Stories to that effect can be found in the miracle legends associated with the major shrines.

An equally compelling motive that took the pilgrim to a sequence of shrines was the search for renewed physical or mental health.[8] The collections of miracle stories supported a deeply-rooted belief that plague, leprosy, tremors, fever, ulcers, toothache, migraine, blindness, deafness and dumbness were visited on the Christian as punishment for his sins. The profession of doctor or surgeon did not inspire such confidence as the intercession of St Thomas, St Eutrope or St James. Most of the great shrines in France along the routes to Santiago were healing-shrines, and as the lists of miracle cures accumulated, each shrine cultivated its speciality. St Lazare of Autun was the patron saint of lepers, St Hugh of Lincoln cured toothache and St Hilaire of Poitiers took care of sufferers from ergot poisoning – a common ailment due to eating rotten grain. These cures, apart from being advertised in books of saints' lives such as the *Golden Legend* (*Legenda Aurea*)[9] were displayed locally in the form of *ex-votos* or offerings of widely-differing quality. In the main they consisted of lead, wooden or wax models of whichever part of the body had been affected. At Santiago those who stood guard over the shrine were told not to accept paltry gifts of cheap models made out of lead or wax.

It is a commonplace of architectural history that the great pilgrimage churches on what were known as the 'major' routes were not only built within the same relatively short period, but that there was a family resemblance in the disposition of the various parts dictated by the need to absorb vast crowds on feast-days and jubilees and to allow circulation round the main and side altars with the minimum interruption to the offices.[10] Indeed the author of the Pilgrim's Guide, Aimery Picaud, drew attention to the resemblance between the

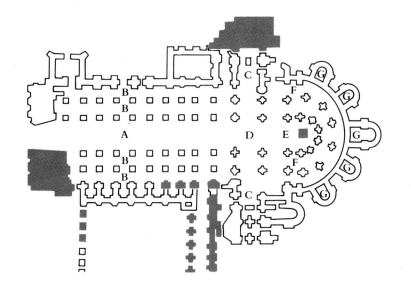

13 *Ground-plan of St Martin de Tours (built 997-1014), showing the typical general shape of a pilgrimage church:* **A** *nave;* **B** *side-aisles;* **C** *transepts;* **D** *crossing;* **E** *apse;* **F** *ambulatory;* **G** *chapels. The shaded areas indicate the surviving sections of the building.*

Cathedral of St James and that of St Martin of Tours in France, without saying which was the original source of inspiration. It is generally accepted that the latter church, built by the treasurer Hervé at Tours between 997 and 1014 laid down the main lines of the pilgrimage church: it had an ambulatory, an apse with radiating chapels and galleries, transepts with side-aisles, and a long nave with double side-aisles (Fig. 13). Nothing beyond a couple of towers survives today. The other pilgrimage churches in general chronological sequence were Ste Foy of Conques, St Martial of Limoges (destroyed), St James of Compostela, and St Sernin of Toulouse.

Building on such a large scale had been rendered possible by the improved conditions for travel from the eleventh century onwards. In the previous two centuries raiders, both Viking and Moor, struck deep into northern Spain, France and the Alps. The overland route to Jerusalem was impossible; in 997 Santiago was sacked and in 1002 the Monastery of San Millán de la Cogolla, which had been the spiritual centre of Castile and Navarre, was destroyed. But in less than a hundred years, as the states of the Christian north drove southwards, such alien penetrations ceased to occur.

The pilgrim routes that took shape as a result of improved security did not differ much from the old Roman roads, though there were deviations where new shrines had sprung up. The maintenance of roads was haphazard and local, and volunteer labour was often summoned by local hermits, who became famous as causeway constructors and bridge-builders. Some of their work survives to the present day, especially in Spain, although in a much remodelled state. The natural hazards were compounded by the professional and amateur brigandage along certain stretches of the route, which became especially acute as the seasonal waves of travellers increased, forcing the pilgrims to travel in convoy. The pilgrim was in general protected by

14 *The crypt of the Basilica of Ste Marie Madeleine, Vézelay. The increase in veneration of Mary Magdalene in France brought about the need for a relic at Vézelay. Early official accounts explain that the saint's remains were brought from the Holy Land by one of the monks of Vézelay. A later version of the* translatio, *as it was technically called, changes the story into another* furtum sacrum *(see Fig. 12), claiming that a monk from Vézelay removed the relics from Aix and bore them back to Vézelay. The reliquary is placed in a ninth-century niche in the crypt, which is the oldest part of the church. Nowadays a seventeenth-century crucifix hangs over a modern altar.*

15 *Figures on the west front of the Cathedral Church of St Trophime, Arles. St Trophime is seen on the right, receiving his mitre from two angels, next to St James in the middle, represented as an evangelist. The cathedral was first dedicated to St Stephen, whose martyrdom is depicted on the opposite side of the doorway, and then to the fifth-century Bishop Trophimos. Most of this building dates from the eleventh and twelfth centuries.*

the law, and ecclesiastical authorities censured those who attacked and robbed and held to ransom those who were dressed as pilgrims. The best protection they could seek was from military orders, which appeared from the early twelfth century when the pilgrimages were well established. These 'soldier' monks, who had taken the monastic vows of poverty, chastity and obedience and funded their operations by giving their possessions to the orders, organized themselves into local units or commanderies, established castles at strong-points for the protection of travellers as well as shepherds and their flocks, and founded hospitals and hostels which they staffed with professionals. Over the years, these orders grew rich on gifts of land and inevitably were drawn into politics and banking. This was particularly true of the Templars, who were accused of unorthodox behaviour and eventually dissolved in 1312.

Hospitality was offered to pilgrims by churchmen and by those religious orders and lay institutions which specialized in that sort of activity. Where monasteries could not accommodate the crowds,

16 *The central porch, Church of St Gilles du Gard, Arles. Little remains of this once magnificent church except the façade and various remnants around the apse. The Golden Legend tells us of its foundation by a young Athenian, Aegidius, who was living in Arles. Repelled by urban life he sought solitude in the forest, where he was fed by wild beasts. Nobles of the ancient Visigothic kingdom, hunting in the region, shot him in the hand by mistake. Their king Wamba insisted on having a monastery founded there in honour of this saintly hermit, of which Gilles (the French form of Aegidius) was to be the abbot. The reliquary of St Gilles became the subject of devotion by pilgrims.*

17 (below) *Detail of Roman sculpture from the necropolis at Alyscamps, Arles. This vast necropolis of stone sarcophagi of both Christian and pagan burials is the source of many legends of martyrs and saints.*

18 (next page) *Landscape, lake and mountains north of Villefort, looking towards Mont Lozère (1,699 metres) in the Massif Central. This is the land traversed by the pilgrim as he moved from the Rhone basin up on to the plateau and headed west to Conques.*

large guest-halls or hostels were set up, often with their own independent administration, either by the Augustinians or the Benedictines, by local noblemen or by royalty, as at the great hospital of Burgos. At the height of the pilgrimage era, a traveller, pilgrim or not, would probably have been able to reach a hostel at the end of every day's journey. There, according to the status of the establishment, he would receive a bed, or straw, food and alms and spiritual succour, for there was usually a chapel attached. In many cases help was reduced simply to shelter. At times the hostel was built astride the road, and the stone-vaulting with benches provided elementary shelter. The pilgrims left their graffiti on the stone blocks in the shape of crosses or horseshoes, just like any traveller (Fig. 11).

19   *This carving from the Church of St Gilles du Gard, Arles, is part of a lintel frieze on three porches that form a remarkable panorama of the life of Christ, a characteristic motif on many churches along the pilgrim route. Despite mutilation, the frieze of the central porch is very sensitive. The detail here shows Christ washing the feet of the apostles. (See Fig. 21)*

20 (below)   *Christ in Majesty, Abbey Church of Ste Foy Conques. This is a detail of the magnificent tympanum constructed in the early twelfth century (see Figs. 24, 25, 28, 136). In the centre is Christ, seated on the clouds, on the Day of Judgement. His right hand welcomes the elect, while his left points downwards to the damned.*

21   *The kiss of Judas, lintel frieze, Church of St Gilles du Gard, Arles. Other scenes in the frieze include Christ expelling the merchants from the temple; the raising of Lazarus; the Last Supper; and Christ carrying the Cross.*

22 *St James (detail), south porch, Cathedral of Notre Dame, Chartres. St James is wearing the customary shell on his robe and carrying the sword with which he was martyred.*

23 (opposite) *Cyclops, south porch, Church of St Pierre d'Aulnay de Saintonge. This Romanesque porch is lush with sculpture and is one of the fascinating delights of the Poitou region. The outer voussoir contains 34 panels of mythological beasts, birds or combinations of man and beast, displaying the profusion of nature's oddities. (See Figs. 32, 38-40)*

24,25 *Two details from the scroll surrounding the arch over the tympanum of the central porch, Abbey Church of Ste Foy, Conques. The scroll divides the magical space of revelation from the daily space of everyday life. At the apex* **(above)** *it is held in the hands of a human figure. He represents the human agents of the great spectacle of the Day of Judgement shown in the tympanum beneath him (Figs. 20, 28), the masons, sculptors, constructors of the masterpiece. This figure acts as a sort of human signature.*
One of the singular features of the tympanum is the way the terror of the Day of Judgement is presented to the audience of pilgrims and others in mesmerized contemplation. Here **(right)** *we have a symbolic figuration of this same audience in the absurdly tiny, shrinking figure of the common man, who appears to have come upon the awesome scene by chance and can scarcely bear to peer over the edge of the scroll at his future.*

26 *Chapel of St Michel d'Aiguilhe, Le Puy en Velay. The charter of this oratory dates from AD 962, though the chapel was enlarged considerably in the twelfth century. The façade contains many Mozarabic traits comparable to those in the nearby cathedral. The trilobed arch in a decorated frieze of lozenges contains an image of the Agnus Dei, flanked by two angels and surrounded by eight elders offering golden cups of perfume symbolizing human prayers.*

The pilgrim prepared for his journey of purification by making amends to his enemies, satisfying his creditors, drawing up his will, deciding any benefactions he thought necessary for the good of his soul, depositing his valuables, and making general confession of his sins. For without sincere confession, according to the *Veneranda Dies*, the journey was useless. Then the pilgrim would seek out his parish priest or bishop to receive formal blessing on himself and on the dress he had adopted. The elements of this dress, which seemed to reach something of the nature of a recognizable uniform by the thirteenth century, consisted of the staff, the tunic, the scrip or pouch and the large broad-brimmed hat, turned up at the front and attached at the back to a long scarf. The *Veneranda Dies* included the formula with

27 *The ambulatory, Chapel of St Michel d'Aiguilhe, Le Puy en Velay. At the rear, lower right, can be seen the entrance to this strange place of prayer. Several stone steps, cut partly into the rock, lead to the sanctuary.*

28 (below) *Tympanum (lower register), Abbey Church of Ste Foy, Conques. In its dimensions, composition and treatment of detail, this is one of the most remarkable of Romanesque tympana. To the left, a series of arcaded columns shelter the saints in Paradise; under the middle arch Abraham receives the souls of the elect; above the double-pitched roof Ste Foy abases herself before God, while angels open the coffins of the dead. In the centre St Michael weighs the souls in the balance; facing him, the devil tries to cheat by leaning on one of the dishes. Hell occupies all the space on the right of the tympanum on various registers. The author of these scenes of violence and torture possesses an extraordinary imagination. All the damned suffer the most excruciating fates, and some of them, as in Dante's Inferno, are identifiable as local figures, both lay and ecclesiastic. One of the most remarkable effects is the expression of the narrow distance between Paradise and Hell, seen here in the timorous backward glance of one of the elect, and the scowling demon with his raised club, deprived of his prey.*

29 *Chapel of St Michel d'Aiguilhe, Le Puy en Velay. The archangel St Michael favours high places—such as St Michael's Mount, Cornwall, England, and Mont-Saint-Michel, Brittany. This volcanic plug measures 82 metres high, 57 metres in diameter and 170 metres round the base. A curious rock formation, it is covered in mosses, mauve irises and golden flowers in the spring, and is a superb foil to the spire of the nearby cathedral. For most of the Middle Ages it was a place of pilgrimage, together with the Chapel of St Gabriel at the base and St Guignefort halfway up. The ascent begins with a Romanesque arch, followed by 268 steps which zig-zag up one side of the pinnacle.*

30 *Mountain landscape seen from the medieval settlement of La Garde Guérin, Massif Central. This heavily reconstructed refuge for modern architects and craftsmen lies near the flank of Mont Lozère on the route to Mende and Conques. The elevated plain could make easy walking for the pilgrim, but there were great stretches of forest and few signs of settlement.*

which the staff and wallet were blessed and handed over to the pilgrim. The ceremony had its origin in the blessing given to the knight (who was very close in status to the pilgrim) departing on the first crusade. The pilgrim also wore certain badges and gathered tokens to show which shrines he had visited, so that the palm was quickly identified with Jerusalem and the scallop-shell with St James. There were also crude representations of St Michael or St Leonard weighing souls at the Last Judgement or freeing captives from their chains. The broad-brimmed hat appeared last of all, in the late thirteenth century, with the front brim turned up and often decorated with a scallop-shell.

In the opening lines of the Pilgrim's Guide in Book Five of the *Liber Sancti Jacobi* the author lays out succinctly the pattern of the roads to St James:

Four are the ways which, going towards Santiago, unite in a single one at Puente la Reina in Spanish territory. One goes through St Gilles, Montpellier, Toulouse and the Somport pass; another by Ste Marie du Puy,

31 *St Martin has the pagan tree cut down; capital, south aisle, Basilica of Ste Marie Madeleine, Vézelay. This church has an unequalled series of nave capitals illustrating incidents from the two Testaments and the lives of the early saints. (See Fig. 33)*

32 *Figures from south porch, Church of St Pierre d'Aulnay de Saintonge. The dramatic character of this porch is enhanced by the deep recession of each of the successive circles of carved figures surmounting the doorway. The series seen here have been sculpted to appear as if supporting the weight of the stone above.*

33 *The mystic mill, Moses and St Paul, capital, south aisle, Basilica of Ste Marie Madeleine, Vézelay. In this symbolic representation of the link between the Old Testament and the New, a figure dressed in a shirt pours grain into a hand-mill while another, barefoot and in a loose garment, recovers the flour. The former is Moses, and the grain stands for the Laws of the Old Testament. The mill which grinds the grain is Christ, and the flour, representing the teachings of the New Testament, is gathered by the apostle Paul.*

34 *Central portal, Basilica of Ste Marie Madeleine, Vézelay. On entering the half-darkness of the narthex, or covered porch, one is struck by the wide avenue of light that stretches away to the sanctuary. This ample narthex was designed for pilgrims to assemble and pause, before moving to the reliquary (Fig. 14) at the east end. It is also known as the 'Galilee porch', because important processions began here, symbolizing the apostles going down to Galilee. Thus this place becomes the transitional passage from profane to sacred. The portal is dominated by a seated Christ, his arms open while the flames of the Holy Spirit shoot down to the apostles on the occasion of Pentecost.*

35 *Landscape near Vézelay. A convent was established near here in about AD 800 by Girart de Rousillon, but Vézelay first achieved real importance in the eleventh century with the arrival of the relics of Mary Magdalene. Many historic figures came here as pilgrims and crusaders.*

36 (below) *Fortified entrance gate to the town of Parthenay. Although Parthenay was not on the direct route from Tours, it was well patronized by pilgrims, who lodged near the rich merchants' lath and timber houses around the main street, Vau St Jacques. The medieval town has been remarkably well preserved and sensitively restored.*

37 (above) *Twelfth-century Church of St Hilaire, Melle. In a niche above the north doorway is a crowned figure on a horse trampling a seated figure. Such statues can frequently be seen in Poitou and elsewhere on the pilgrim route. It is generally assumed that they were erected to honour the Emperor Constantine, who in the Edict of Milan (AD 313) established the supremacy of Christianity over paganism.*

38,39 *Church of St Pierre d'Aulnay de Saintonge. The right tympanum of the south porch* **(above right)** *depicts Christ in Majesty flanked by two unidentified figures. In the interior of the church is a series of heavily incised capitals, displaying foliage, grotesque heads and elephants* **(right)**. *In medieval bestiaries the elephant stood for temperance and sovereignty.*

40 *Church of St Pierre d'Aulnay de Saintonge. Above the south porch are three arcaded blind windows. This is one of four twelfth-century warriors, armed with spears and pointed shields, ingeniously carved on the face and underside of the arch over the central window.*

Ste Foy de Conques and St Pierre de Moissac; the third goes through Ste Marie Madeleine de Vézelay, St Leonard du Limousin and the town of Périgueux; another runs by St Martin of Tours, St Hilaire of Poitiers, St Jean d'Angély, St Eutrope of Saintes and the town of Bordeaux. The roads which pass through Ste Foy, St Leonard and St Martin come together at Ostabat, and after crossing the Port de Cize, meet up in Puente la Reina with one that crosses the Somport pass. From here a single road leads to Santiago.

Thus the process of constant travel which began on the Roman roads and commercial portways settled down, with few deviations, into a pattern joining up the principal pilgrimage sanctuaries. It spread across France like an outstretched hand with the wrist resting on the western Pyrenees, and along the fingers lay the shrines which the Guide recommended the pilgrim to visit.

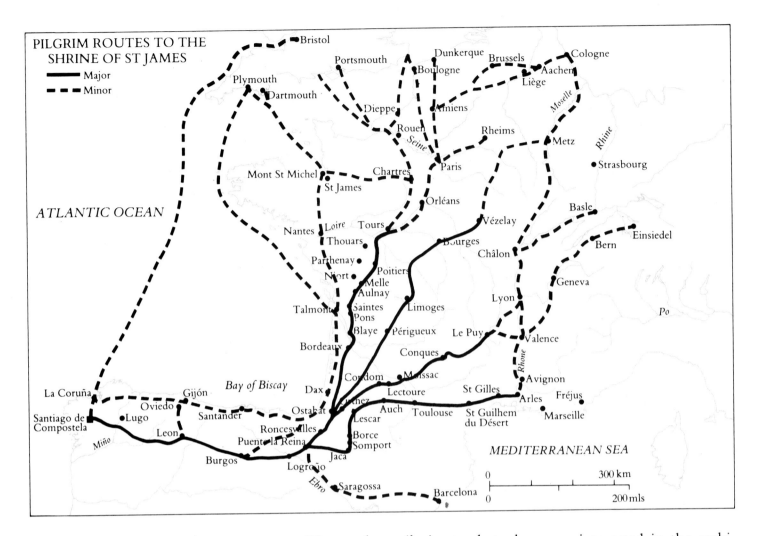

PILGRIM ROUTES TO THE SHRINE OF ST JAMES

— Major

- - - Minor

41 *Across medieval France four major pilgrimage routes converged on the Pyrenees. Two main crossings at Roncesvalles and Somport carried the routes across the mountains to meet at Puente la Reina. From there a single route continued to Santiago de Compostela.*

The modern pilgrim tends to be more interested in the architecture and decoration than the original reasons why these churches were constructed. He has often little knowledge of the dedication of the church or the special characteristics of the saint involved. Yet much can be learned about early spirituality from the imagined activities of these shadowy figures. In the majority of cases we are dealing with men and women from the periods of persecution and evangelization (third to fourth centuries), of pagan stock, converted in dramatic circumstances to become hermits and to withdraw to obscure and distant refuges in forests, now the locations of their sanctuary. Some of these figures were held to be powerful in their lifetime, but their abiding authority derives from their posthumous sanctity. Some can be identified with historical figures; others, like the epic heroes of later secular poetry, are pure invention, but not totally free fantasy. Their actions reinforce beliefs and convictions which the age deemed important; the narrative stories of their lives became sources of admiration and shock.

Let us now trace the four main routes through France, from their initial points at Arles, Le Puy, Vézelay and Tours.

Starting at the Cathedral of St Trophime in Arles the pilgrims of the time of Aimery Picaud would not have seen the present west façade, where St Trophime features prominently with the apostles, including St James the Great and St James the Less (Fig. 15). Instead they would pass on through the celebrated necropolis of Alyscamps (Fig. 17) to the Church of St Honorat, a fifth-century Bishop of Arles. Sarcophagi, lined up in a long perspective closed by the octagonal church tower, carry here and there the sign of the Cross and the chrism or Holy Oil. Only a few miles away is the infinitely superior sanctuary of St Gilles du Gard (Figs. 16, 19, 21). The romantic story of this supposed Athenian youth, who inexplicably turned up in Arles and abandoned urban life to seek a refuge in the forest, is contained in the *Golden Legend*, but the magnificent tomb relic in marble and gold which Aimery Picaud had visited has disappeared. It worked remarkable miracles because, according to Aimery, the body of the Saint was complete, a feature shared by only three other saints, of whom another was St James the Great. The third stage is at St Guilhem du Désert, where the epic hero Count Guillaume Fierabras, relative of Charlemagne, widower of a Moorish princess, bridge-builder and

42 *This twelfth-century hospital arch outside the town walls of Pons joined the old hospital and the chapel, neither of which have survived. The arch provided shelter for pilgrims. They could rest on the stone benches that flank the tunnel, and even leave their dead in the hollowed-out sarcophagi.*

43 *Twelfth-century Church of Ste Radegonde, Talmont. The fishing village of Talmont lies on the eastern side of the estuary of the Garonne. Pilgrims came here by land and by sea, across the Bay of Biscay from England. The squat little Romanesque church was once contained within a fortified redoubt, but the wall has now mostly fallen away. It is still a mariners' church, with ex-votos recalling sailors and the sea. In the days of the medieval pilgrimage it would certainly have been full of trifling offerings in lead and jet, left by those who had just faced the rough seas of the bay, and those who were about to do so.*

warrior turned saint, is buried in the abbey he founded. The fourth saint, St Saturninus (or St Sernin) is housed in Toulouse, in one of the most formally representative of the pilgrimage churches. He also was a missionary martyr connected with Spain. After this the pilgrim continued by way of Auch and Lescar to the Somport Pass in the Pyrenees.

The Guide found nothing of importance on the second route, to the north of the first, apart from the sanctuary of Ste Foy of Conques (Figs. 9, 12, 20, 24, 25, 28). (The Church of Notre Dame and the Chapel of St Michel d'Aiguilhe at le Puy, further to the east where the pilgrim road began, are not even mentioned; Figs. 26, 27, 29.) But the situation of the Abbey Church of Ste Foy makes this one of the most dramatic of all the pilgrimage routes. It is set on a mass of red lava stone amongst a tight network of green valleys in the southern Massif Central. Inside the church there is one of the few nearly complete antique reliquary statues, begemmed and enthroned (Fig. 10). The Saint wears a solid crown of ancient form; long earrings reach her shoulders; in each hand she holds two small tubes which once held a model of the bronze bed on which she was roasted. If a plague devastated the area, or a dispute blew up between authorities, Ste Foy's statue was placed upon a horse and taken forth, surrounded by young priests blowing ivory horns. After Conques, the Guide mentions only the famous Church of St Pierre de Moissac, with its majestic west porch. From Moissac the road goes towards Lectoure and Condom, coming finally to Ostabat at the foot of the Pyrenees.

The third route, slanting across the very centre of France, was perhaps the most varied. The flow of pilgrims to visit the remains of Ste Marie Madeleine at Vézelay was already at its height when the Guide was written, but when the pious theft which was supposed to have brought the relics to Vézelay was in turn discovered to be a pious lie, the shrine went into swift decline (Figs. 14, 31, 33, 34). The next sanctuary on the route, that of St Leonard of Noblat, lasted longer because he was the patron saint of prisoners; the Guide marvels at the thousands of iron chains, fetters, leg-irons, left as offerings. The most famous church of all on this route, St Martial of Limoges, is not even mentioned in the Guide, and the present-day pilgrim has to imagine it, for it does not exist today. The road then crosses the Garonne at La Réole to join the route from Le Puy at Ostabat.

The fourth route, from Tours, was the longest, but it was over the easiest terrain, and was better serviced than the others. Perhaps because he knew it best, Aimery Picaud turned this most westerly branch into an impressive procession of saints. In this case it is not only grandiose figures from the dim period of the persecutions, but also knights from the time of Charlemagne who appear, martyrs in defence of the faith against the Moorish invasion. The link between the road to Santiago and the campaigns of Charlemagne is well illustrated by the Cathedral of Chartres, beyond Tours to the north. Here there are half-a-dozen stained-glass windows alluding to St James

(Figs. 6, 7). A pair in the choir, next to the entrance to the treasury, place side by side St James's life and martyrdom and his call to Charlemagne in a vision to proceed to Spain and recover it from the infidel. But Aimery begins the route proper with St Martin of Tours and St Hilaire of Poitiers, pupil and master of the fourth century.

South of Tours the routes are scattered with the remnants of the pilgrims' passage. The roads were easy and the countryside rich and fertile. Parthenay le Vieux still preserves the characteristics of a walled town, with its fortified entrance guarding the bridge over the Thouet, leading to the inns and hostels of the Vau St Jacques within (Fig. 36). The churches at St Pierre d'Aulnay and St Hilaire in Melle offer displays of stone carving, reliefs and statuary in porches and capitals to astound, amuse and instruct the traveller (Figs. 23, 32, 37–40), while south of Saintes, outside the cliff-like fortifications of Pons, there still survive the remains of an impressive hospital in stone of the late twelfth and thirteenth centuries. The three spans of vaulting which bridge the road originally joined hospital and chapel, both of

44 *Crypt and tomb of St Eutrope, Church of St Eutrope, Saintes. Saintes, situated on the River Charente, had been an important fording point for the north-south route from prehistoric times. The double church of St Eutrope was consecrated in 1096 and the oldest and best preserved element of that period is the crypt. Aimery Picaud claims that St Eutrope was the son of the Emir of Babylon. On witnessing the miracle of the loaves and fishes, he received the Holy Spirit and was despatched (like so many others mentioned in the Pilgrim's Guide) to southern France by St Peter. He was martyred at Saintes, and in subsequent years his body healed the sick and set prisoners free. His remains lie in a simple sarcophagus in the crypt.*

which are now gone, but the stone tunnel remains can still shelter the pilgrim (Fig. 42).

Aimery's support for relics near his homeland reaches a climax with St Eutrope of Saintes (Fig. 44), probably the most spurious of all the saints mentioned so far, and for whom Aimery produces the greatest quantity of proof, in the form of a Greek document brought back by him from Constantinople which he inserted in its totality into the Guide. As one approaches the Pyrenees the shrines begin to recall not the legendary missions to convert the pagans, but the relatively more recent figure of Charlemagne and his campaigns against the Moors. They say the body of Roland lies in the Church of St Romain in the estuary of the Garonne; at Belin are revered the bodies of his knights, Oliver, Ogier, Garin, etc. And at St Seurin in Bordeaux is to be found the oliphant or horn of Roland.

The four main routes that lead to the Pyrenees do not, of course, start precisely at the points mentioned in the Guide. As the years passed, many minor roads flowed into Arles, Le Puy, Vézelay and Tours. Paris itself was linked up with the Low Countries; London, Weymouth, Dartmouth, Bristol trafficked with the French channel ports. An alternative route for English sea-travellers led to the fishing port of Talmont in the Garonne estuary, overlooked by the twelfth-century Church of Ste Radegonde, hung with offerings of ships (Fig. 43). Or one could take a boat straight to the north coast of Spain, to the Basque ports, or Asturias, or Galicia. These voyages were testing and uncomfortable, and probably exposed pilgrims to more dangers than land routes, but they were not discouraged in some cases from combining the long trip by sea and land to Santiago with the even more hazardous one to Jerusalem.

45 *Intertwined cats and birds, capital, Parish Church of Chadenac. This church, constructed about 1150, is called the Marchioness of Saintonge on account of its architectural charm. The sculpture on the main doorway is of high quality, representing the theme of the Virtues and the Vices, a favourite motif of the pilgrimage church.*

II † Across the Pyrenees

Progress across France towards the Pyrenees was comparatively easy for the pilgrim. The rivers were fordable and there were no major natural obstacles to overcome. He was cared for at intervals by hospital, monastery and guild, and his progress was unimpeded by the peasantry. Such, at least, is the testimony of Aimery Picaud, who came by the most prosperous route. The situation began to change as the pilgrim approached the territory bordering the northern flank of the Pyrenees. The Atlantic coastal strip was flat, marshy, unproductive and infested with flies; and having penetrated this area inhabited by the Basques, the pilgrim had to contend with uncongenial natives who fought as much amongst themselves as they did with foreigners. This was perhaps inevitable in people who had been continually beset by immigrants and emigrants since prehistoric times. For the Pyrenees, while visibly presenting a solid barrier of parallel mountain ranges between the Iberian Peninsula and the rest of Europe, have never been a serious obstacle to the movement of people from north to south, or vice versa.

There was a significant increase in this traffic between the eleventh and thirteenth centuries to which the movement of pilgrims only partly contributed. North of the Pyrenees, Europe was undergoing a period of transformation, seen in the growth of towns and trade. This coincided with far-reaching reforms within the Church, instigated by the Benedictine abbots of Cluny in France. South of the Pyrenees, the Caliphate of Cordoba had fragmented into a series of independent states by the middle of the eleventh century, and Moorish power in the western Mediterranean had dramatically diminished. Amongst the Christian states, Navarre at the western end of the Pyrenees was initially most responsive to the changes taking place in Europe. Sancho the Great (*el Mayor*, 1000-35) and his successors established marriage links with the French. It was Sancho who sent the hermit Paternus to Cluny to extend the discipline of Cluny to Navarre. He was also responsible for creating the kingdom of Castile, which he gave his son Fernando; his other son Ramiro became the first king of Aragon. The expanding Christian principalities needed manpower and material for their first significant thrust southwards against the Moors, and along the pilgrims' roads they offered easy terms to

46 *Museum of the Benedictine Monastery at Cluny. The Abbey of Cluny is not on the route to Compostela, but the influence of its monks and of its architecture were felt throughout the breadth of Christendom. It provided popes, prelates and abbots to a multitude of institutions. More than 10,000 monks observed its rule. Its greatest abbot was St Hugh. When he died in 1109, the order was at the zenith of its influence, and the links that were established with the monarchs of northern Spain had an inevitable impact on the pilgrimage to Compostela. After the French Revolution in 1798, the authorities started to sell off the Cluny property piecemeal. These columns and capitals, re-assembled in the flour barn, or farinier, surround the old altar of Pyrenean marble blessed by Pope Urban II in 1096. Their capitals reveal the first signs of Burgundian Romanesque, which was to spread to Autun and Vézelay.*

travellers to tempt them to settle as privileged foreigners or Franks (as they came to be called). Special suburbs were built for them around the major towns along the route. In the eleventh century there were more foreigners in Pamplona than natives, and Estella in Navarre was founded exclusively for French settlers.

Although as we have seen in the previous chapter, legend makes of Charlemagne the first pilgrim and crusader, and attributes to him the freedom of the pilgrim route, no hard evidence of pilgrim itineraries appears before the eleventh century. Some people argue for early routes along the coast, but there are weighty geographical and social arguments against this. It is only with the reign of Sancho the Great

47 *Roof vaulting, Abbey Church of St Peter and St Paul, Benedictine Monastery, Cluny. When in 1130 Abbot Peter the Venerable completed the church begun by St Hugh, it served 460 monks and was the largest church in Christendom until St Peter's in Rome was rebuilt. The interior was 177 metres in length (St Peter's measures 186 metres), with five naves, two transepts, five bell towers and two towers. The only fragments of this church that remain are the southern apse and the two towers. These are examples of Burgundian Romanesque in its purest state.*

that data start to accrue. Following him the main architects of the route are Alfonso VI of Leon and Castile (1065-1109) and Sancho Ramírez I of Navarre and Aragon (1063-94). The former announced his intention of repairing all the bridges from Logroño to Compostela and the latter forbade his subjects to tax pilgrims who crossed the mountains to Jaca and Pamplona. By the middle of the next century the route had come to correspond with that described in Book V of the *Liber Sancti Jacobi*, and already from the end of the eleventh the term *via jacobea* appeared in documents as its name.

As the general map of the routes indicates, those pilgrims who followed the southern route from Toulouse through Auch, Lescar and

48 *Evening sun over the mountains above the Pyrenean village of Borce, a tiny slate-roofed settlement at the beginning of the first stage of the pilgrim route over the Somport pass.*

Sorde l'Abbaye

1 Indicates end of stage in journey
as given by the *Liber Sancti Jacobi*

Scale 1:600000

0   30 km
0   20 mls

St Palais
St Sauveur
(Gibraltar)
Harambels
Ostabat
Larceveau

Oloron

Nive

St Jean Pied
de Port
St Michel le Vieux

G. d'Oloron

Saison

VALLÉE D'ASPE

Valcarlos

San Salvador
de Ibañeta
Roncesvalles
Burguete

1 Viscarret

FRANCE
SPAIN

Borce

P   Y   R   E   N   E   E   S

Larrasoaña

Arga

Irati

VALLE DE IRATI

Esca

VALLE DEL RONCAL

Somport
Santa Cristina

2

Cizur Menor

Pamplona

N   A   V   A   R   R   E

Salaza

VALLE DE HECHO

Canfranc

Erro

Monreal

Óbanos
Eunate
Puente la Reina

Arga

illatuerta

Foz de
Lumbier

Leyre

Aragón

Veral

Aragón

Jaca

Sangüesa

Puente de la
Reina de Aragón

Santa Cruz de Serós

San Juan de la Peña

50   *Landscape between San Juan de la
Peña and Jaca, ploughed fields and
pasture.*

Fig. 49

Across the Pyrenees

51,52 *These sculptures depict Adam* **(above)**, *and Christ and the woman taken in adultery* **(right)**. *They are part of a series of twelfth-century capitals illustrating scenes from the Old and New Testaments, in the cloisters of the Lower Monastery of San Juan de la Peña.*

Oloron began the first major stage of the great voyage at the Pyrenean village of Borce (Fig. 48). From there began the long climb up the wooded slopes to the famous Hospital of Santa Cristina at the summit, or Somport; after that the descent followed the rocky valley of the River Aragón to Jaca and its remarkable cathedral. Santa Cristina was called by *Liber Sancti Jacobi* 'loca sancta, domus Dei' ('a holy place, the mansion of the Lord'), one of the three necessary supports for pilgrims in Europe, of which the other two were the hospital in Jerusalem and that on the great St Bernard's Pass in the Alps. It lay to the right of the present road, before the bridge of Santa Cristina. Regretfully nothing of it remains today beyond a few crumbled walls.

53,54 *Daniel's vision* **(left)**; *a supplicating figure* **(above)**. *Capitals in the cloisters of the Lower Monastery of San Juan de la Peña. The Lower Monastery is thrust into a cleft at the base of an overhanging precipice (peña) in a mountain valley. It was here that the first kings of Aragon established their pantheon, consecrated in 1094. There are two churches in the Lower Monastery, one on top of the other. The lower storey, with its Mozarabic church cut into the rock, is probably tenth-century; the one above, to which the pantheon and cloisters are attached, is late eleventh-century. Only two galleries remain.*

Jaca, standing high on a neck of land above the river valley and overlooked by the Peña de Oroel was, until relatively recently, a walled town. It reached a peak of political authority in the eleventh century when it became the capital of the new kingdom of Aragon under its first king, Ramiro I (1035-63). In structural terms the Cathedral of Jaca is a significant monument to the cultural cross-play of that period. From Jaca the road followed the line of the River Aragón to the west, crossing it at Puente de la Reina de Aragón (not to be confused with its namesake in Navarre). On the northern side of the modern reservoir of Yesa, thrust into a fold of the Pyrenean foothills, under great walls of ochre-coloured stone, squats the

56 *Crypt, consecrated 1057, of the Monastery Church of San Salvador de Leyre. San Salvador was used by Sancho the Great of Navarre and his successors as a burial place. Later the kings of Aragon used San Juan de la Peña. San Salvador is just off the pilgrim route as it traverses the Ebro valley to Puente la Reina.*

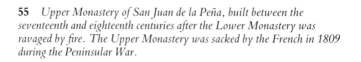

55 *Upper Monastery of San Juan de la Peña, built between the seventeenth and eighteenth centuries after the Lower Monastery was ravaged by fire. The Upper Monastery was sacked by the French in 1809 during the Peninsular War.*

57 *The Funerary Chapel of Eunate. Bones found near the exterior arcade support the theory that pilgrims were buried here. The outside gallery was presumably once covered, however no firm conclusions about its use have yet been established. Like the Holy Sepulchre in Jerusalem, the chapel is octagonal in shape, with irregular sides, from one of which projects a semi-circular apse.*

Monastery of San Salvador de Leyre, one of the first Benedictine foundations in Spain. The present building was consecrated in 1057 (Fig. 56). Its crypt is so robust and massive that it looks much older than the structure it was built to sustain. The vaulting is high enough to be bridged by arches with vast keystones and double ribs resting on archaic capitals at knee height. On the southern side of the monastery, at the bottom of the rocky incline, lies the pilgrim road in the valley of the River Aragón, its eroded marl slopes crested with limestone. South-east of San Salvador and south of Jaca, tucked into the base of a cliff, is the monastery of San Juan de la Peña, the burial place of Aragonese kings after San Salvador (Figs. 51-5). The crypt is of the tenth century, while the church is Romanesque, dedicated in 1094. A later monastery was constructed on the summit of the cliff in the seventeenth and eighteenth centuries.

Although the *Liber Sancti Jacobi* does not mention the fact, many pilgrims left the road to turn southwards to Sangüesa, which was being resettled at the time the Guide was being written. Alfonso I of Aragon gave his palace near the bridge over the River Aragón, together with the church of Santa María, to the military order of Hospitallers, and inside the church today an image of Our Lady of Roca-madour recalls this French connection. Further on, the pilgrim road crossed the Irati, a tributary of the River Ebro, over a single-arch bridge (now collapsed) in the narrow and terrifying gorge of the Foz

58 *Stele, seen from above, at St Sauveur, south of St Palais, where five pilgrim roads join and continue south to Ostabat. The mount to the stele is modern, and indicates the directions of the five routes.*

59 *Stepping-stones at a ford over the River Bidouze at Quinquil, used by pilgrims on their way to Ostabat via St Sauveur. The foliage has grown up around the river edge, and the ford is little used now so that it is hard to find from the modern road.*

60 *Remains of undercroft and storage chambers, largely destroyed in the sixteenth century, at the Benedictine Monastery of Sorde l'Abbaye, on the Gave d'Oloron, south west of Peyrehorade. According to legend, this abbey is one of the many possible burial places of the fighting Bishop Turpin, who accompanied Charlemagne on his expedition to Spain against the Moors. The chronicle attributed to Turpin, Book IV of the* Liber Sancti Jacobi, *also reports that Charlemagne built a church near here with gold brought from Spain.*

61,62 *Cathedral of Ste Marie, Oloron. On the tympanum* **(above)** *the twenty-four Elders of the Apocalypse from the Revelation of St John are depicted playing musical instruments. This motif, expressing praise, harmony and joy, is often found above the main door of churches and cathedrals. At the base of the column of the central doorway* **(left)** *is a pair of Moors in chains, servants of the Devil.*

63,64 *Daniel in the lion's den* (**left**), *and an acrobat?* (**above**), *from the Benedictine Abbey of La Sauve Majeure, founded near Bordeaux by St Gerard of Corbie in 1077. Sauve Majeure is derived from* Silva Mayor, *meaning 'Great Forest'. The abbey was an important point of departure for many pilgrims who came here to have their traditional staff and scrip blessed. The staff was the pilgrim's only support and defence; the scrip was used for alms and food. The abbey is now in ruins, but the choir capitals survive, of which these are examples.*

de Lumbier, then swung south of Pamplona past the Castle of Monreal and the octagonal chapel at Eunate to Puente la Reina in Navarre. Scholars suggest that this strange Romanesque building, isolated in the wheatfields (Fig. 57), was a funerary chapel like that of San Salvador in the village of Torres del Río, a little further on.

By far the most travelled and, relatively speaking, the easiest route across the Pyrenees Mountains lay further west through the valley of Valcarlos or up the nearby mountain flank to the Port de Cise. The starting point where all the routes converged from Tours, Vézelay, Le Puy was further north in the foothills, in an area between St Palais and Ostabat. Aimery Picaud does indicate this latter village as the focal point, but examination of the territory reveals that the roads met on a low hill called today St Sauveur or Gibraltar (Fig. 58). It has nothing to do with the famous Rock. The pilgrims had filtered down

65 *Ruined chapel of St Sebastian, near Larceveau, lower Navarre. This originally belonged to a commandery of the Knights of St John. There is no road to the ruin, only a footpath.*

66 *Sixteenth-century roof-painting of sun and moon from the Chapel of St Nicolas in the hamlet of Harambels. The medieval community here offered lodgings to the pilgrims travelling south from St Palais to St Jean Pied de Port.*

through a network of local routes, seeking support and sustenance in the hospitals of the abbeys at La Sauve Majeure (Figs. 63, 64), or Sorde (Fig. 60), or Oloron (Figs. 61, 62), or L'Hôpital St Blaise, fording rivers like the Gave de Pau or the Gave d'Oloron, and little streams like the Bidouze at Quinquil (Fig. 59). They could now see the Pyrenees ahead and were proceeding through undulating territory which was mainly sheep pasture, thinly populated.

When the pilgrims arrived at St Jean Pied de Port they could calculate broadly on a two-month trip to Santiago and back over the seven-hundred odd kilometres of the older route; it had been done in less. They were faced first with a choice of routes on the south side of the River Nive which runs through St Jean. They could veer to the right and follow the Valcarlos valley up to the col at San Salvador de Ibañeta; or they could go to the left, through St Michel le Vieux, up the mountain slope to the crest of Port de Cise and drop slowly to join the other route at San Salvador. The pilgrim, looking back at this point, would see a familiar phenomenon, fresh green valleys and deciduous trees, meadows and pasture criss-crossed with streams. Facing south, however, his eye would strike bare rock and dusty plain. Nothing remains now of the edifices and hospitals associated originally with either route up to the col. Fragments of scallop-shell with holes bored through them can still be picked up today. A piece of a Roman altar to a sun-god is testimony to the ancient existence of the road and the col it passes over. At this point in 1071 was founded the Chapel of San Salvador de Ibañeta. It has been destroyed and rebuilt many times since, and it is here that the pilgrim first faces the province of Galicia, and is expected to plant a cross and make his first prayer to St James. Here, at the westernmost end, the journey begins in the atmosphere of the old epic legends, for in the times of Aimery Picaud a cross, the *Crux Caroli*, stood here and reminded the traveller of the sorrowful tragedy of Roland at Roncesvalles:

Then to the Dale of Rouncevale hit is the waie,
A derk passage I der well saie:
Witelez there ben full necessary,
For in that passage my mouth was dry.
Beyond the hull upon hee…
…the well of Rouland, and Olivier therein.[2]

The present hermitage was built in 1965 in Holy Year and the present cross recalls the one that Charlemagne planted when he turned to call on the aid of St James.

At the foot of the col, a mere mile or so further down amongst the pines lies a group of ecclesiastical buildings at Roncesvalles, and a step or two further, at Burguete, present-day hotels rest on the foundations of old hospitals. First one comes upon the old hospital, called by the Guide *Hospitale Rotolandi* (of Roland), built by Sancho de Larrosa, Bishop of Pamplona in 1132. From its foundation until today it was run by a chapter of regular Austin canons, and in the

67 (opposite) *St James as a pilgrim, with scrip and scallop-shell, Church of San Cernín (St Saturninus), Pamplona. The scallop-shell is associated with the seashore on the Atlantic coast, where the body of St James was landed. It eventually became the symbol of the pilgrim to Santiago.*

68 *Valley of the River Arga in the early morning light, viewed from Alto del Perdón. This is the highest point on the road before the descent towards Puente la Reina.*

69 *Royal Collegiate Church of Nuestra Señora de Roncesvalles. At one time there was a hospital for pilgrims on the north side of the church.*

70 *Street of la Rúa, Estella. Pilgrims crossed the River Ega to enter Estella, and, following along this street, arrived at the Plaza de San Martín, where they would find accommodation.*

seventeenth century it served up to 25,000 meals a year to pilgrims. The collegiate church, Nuestra Señora de Roncesvalles, is nearby (Fig. 69). It was founded by Sancho the Strong who is buried with his wife in the old chapter house, now called the Chapel of St Augustine. Next comes a small single-nave thirteenth-century chapel dedicated to St James. On the south side lies the oldest building of the group in the shape of a square topped by a cupola. It was called either the Church of the Holy Spirit or the *Silo de Carlomagno*, after the medieval tradition that the bodies of Charlemagne's knights once rested there. It was, in fact, a funeral chapel for the pilgrims who died in the hospital, and its cupola probably originally carried a small lantern opening.

The route south follows a fairly gentle slope. The settlements strung out along the valley of the River Arga have little to offer today, half-rural and half-industrial in uneven, untidy patches. According to

71 *Roland fighting the giant Ferragut, capital from the twelfth-century Palace of the Kings of Navarre, Estella. Ferragut is first mentioned in the Chronicle of Bishop Turpin and is also documented elsewhere. A Syrian giant, he had the strength of forty men, and was the lord of Nájera.*

72 (below) *Cloisters, Benedictine Monastery of Irache. The monastery is one of the most ancient in Navarre. It became a university in 1569, when this Renaissance cloister and various other buildings were added.*

73 *Puente la Reina, the pilgrim bridge over the River Arga, where the roads from Roncesvalles and Somport converge. There is an old legend that at long intervals an unidentified bird used to appear nearby, go down to the river, wet its wings and flutter up to clean the statue of the Virgin that stood on the balustrade of the bridge (now removed).*

74 *Landscape near Villamayor, through which the pilgrim route passes. Here we see stubble fields and land ploughed for winter wheat. All this region echoes with epic medieval legends of strife and violence between the Franks and the Navarrese, and the troubles continued right into the nineteenth century with the Carlist Wars.*

75 *Monastery Church, Benedictine Monastery of Irache. The church is Transitional Gothic with Romanesque apses and Gothic naves (see also Fig. 72). From Irache the road to Compostela runs between the heights of Montejurra and Monjardín.*

the Guide, Viscarret is the end of the first stage of the route, placed some thirty-five kilometres from St Michel le Vieux. The second stage of the route ends at Pamplona, under whose ramparts the medieval road curved round to the right, while the modern access to the city is on the left. The pilgrims cross the River Arga over a single-arch bridge in the Magdalena quarter, where once there functioned a hospital for lepers and a refuge for those who could not make the climb to the gates before they closed at night. Above, the gates of France and Zumalacarreguí (a hero of the Peninsular War) lead into the walled section of the city on the northern side. Over the ramparts rises the hump of the cathedral nave and the sharp silhouette of the apse, with its superb cloister on the left. This is much the best approach since on the western side the late eighteenth-century neo-classical façade blanks off from view the pure fourteenth-century structure of the cathedral.

Pamplona has commanded the frontier routes as a political capital from Roman times, with moments of real grandeur, as in the eleventh century when it was the capital of Sancho the Great. Its major expansion came about when this monarch encouraged immigration from beyond the Pyrenees. As can be imagined, this action was not entirely welcomed by the resident population. It led to commerical prosperity but also to continuous feuding between the older quarter near the cathedral, known as the Navarrería, where the local inhabitants lived, and the newer quarters of San Cernín and San Nicolás settled by the foreigners or Franks, where the pilgrims lodged. From the eleventh century onwards the religious and public service institutions grew to meet the continuous traffic. The original Romanesque cathedral, of which only fragments remain in the city museum, was expanded. The

76 *Dome and vaulting in the twelfth-century octagonal Church of Santo Sepulcro, Torres del Río. The rib pattern is similar to that used in Moorish Spain, and it was exported to churches on the other side of the Pyrenees, such as St Croix in Oloron.*

Hospital of San Miguel, beside the cathedral, contained some fifty beds and offered the pilgrim bread, wine, root and green vegetables and meat. The pilgrim seeking further for lodgings or food descended from the cathedral along the Calle de los Mercaderes through the original gates to the suburbs of San Nicolás and San Cernín. The fourteenth-century church here, dedicated to St Saturninus, still carries on its blackened façade an image of St James with his cockle-shell (Fig. 67). At his feet, a pilgrim prays for his protection. Opposite the church stood another hospital. The pilgrim's route then curved onwards past the quarter of San Lorenzo, also with a hospital, and led him into the third stage of the journey ending at Estella.

Leaving Pamplona by the Calle Fuente de Hierro along the old Roman road, the pilgrim climbed the Sierra del Perdón, turning off to the left to pass through the village of Cizur Menor. This held an important commandery of the Hospitallers in the twelfth century; today one can only glimpse the interior of the Romanesque church, now turned into a barn and a hayloft in imminent danger of collapse. The pilgrim road then wanders upwards, to the left of the main road, often disappearing into the undergrowth, to the highest point of the ridge, known as the Alto del Perdón, where one is rewarded finally by a magnificent panorama of the Arga valley patterned with rich and luscious meadows, lines of poplars, vineyards and small villages like Óbanos where the road from Somport joins up, just before Puente la Reina (Fig. 68).

Here, as the River Arga swings north across the route to flow into the River Ebro, the pilgrim encounters the first major river crossing and the *raison d'être* of Puente la Reina (Fig. 73). The six-arched bridge has changed little through the centuries, and is likely to change little in the future, relieved as it is of all wheeled traffic by the nearby steel-framed modern substitute. And the little town has not changed much structurally, with its long box-like perimeter bisected by the main street. It owes its name to a woman who may be either the queen of Sancho the Great, or her granddaughter, who caused the bridge to be built in the late eleventh century for travellers and prospective settlers.

The real advocates of settlement were, however, Alfonso I, King of Aragon, and García VI of Navarre in the following century. García put the town in the hands of the Templars in 1142 and instructed them to help the pilgrims 'for the love of God' and for nothing else. The Hospital of the Crucifix, outside the main gate to the town on the east, was built in the mid-fifteenth century on the site of a Templar foundation. One can still see the remains, with the entrance to the old hospital on the left of the road as one approaches Puente la Reina, and the chapel on the right, both joined overhead, as at Pons or Sorde, by a spacious vault. A doorway gives entry to a Romanesque barrel-vaulted, single-nave chapel parallel to which runs a Gothic chapel containing the tomb of the founder, Juan de Beaumont, and a wooden Christ of the late fourteenth century of German origin, hung on a Y-shaped Cross. This has given the hospital the local name of Hospital del Crucifigo. Further down, the main-road traffic thunders past the end of the ill-paved street and across the way can be seen, built into the adjacent buildings, the two towers flanking the original gate to the town. Halfway down the Calle Mayor de los Romeus lies the Church of St James with a fine south-entrance arch of the late twelfth century.

Estella sits on a gorge of the River Ega, another tributary of the Ebro, a crossing-point from north to south and east to west, halfway between Pamplona and Logroño, with half-a-dozen churches and monasteries propped on its rocky slopes and thankfully bypassed by modern traffic. The traffic roars up above through a tunnel bored through the shoulder of the Montejurra. But this town did not grow up slowly. It was deliberately invented in the late eleventh century, the road altered to run through it, and settled practically exclusively by foreigners on royal invitation from its foundation in 1090. One could still hear Provençal being spoken in the streets in the fourteenth century, and the foreign atmosphere in the place is manifest in its names. The quarter where the Franks and the Jews were located is crossed by the main street, la Rúa (Fig. 70), and the first church one meets is that of the Holy Sepulchre, blackened and eroded, with a magnificent fourteenth-century Gothic façade and a St James at the flank of the entrance. There are two hermitages with dedications to the French shrines of Notre Dame du Puy and Rocamadour. The Plaza de San Martín is the commercial centre and the quarter where the pilgrims stayed. The church of the same name lies opposite the Royal Palace of the Kings of Navarre, with its excellent façade and the carved capital bearing the image of Roland fighting the giant Ferragut with a sword (Fig. 71). The pilgrims left by the Gate of San Nicolás.

77 (opposite) *View of Lower Monastery of San Millán de la Cogolla, as seen from the Upper Monastery. In the sixteenth century the monks abandoned the earlier Upper Monastery for this more convenient location near the river. This edifice too now stands virtually empty, its famous relics and documents moved to Madrid, including the first written example of the Castilian language, in interlinear translations of the Bible. But the monastery still possesses vast altar paintings by Fr. Juan Rizi on the life and miracles of St James.*

78 *Monastery of Santa María la Real, Nájera (founded 1052). The delicate stonework seen here in the cloisters (1520) is known as plateresque. It is characteristic of external decoration of secular and religious buildings in Castile at the turn of the fifteenth/sixteenth centuries.*

Before the foundation of Estella, travellers passed directly from Villatuerta, just east of the town, up the steep slope on the left of the Montejurra peak to the Benedictine Monastery and Hospital of Irache, heading for Nájera, the end of stage four of the route.

Irache was amongst the oldest Benedictine foundations in Navarre, and a hospital was founded here by García as early as 1051–4. The walls of this edifice can still be seen embedded in one of the massive courtyards of the later buildings which stand today, gaunt, empty and echoing. The monastery church is a spacious, lofty and restrained Romanesque edifice restored in 1942 (Figs. 72, 75). A little further down the road on the southern side is something of quite a different scale and origin. In the village of Torres del Río is perched the little monastery church of the Order of the Holy Sepulchre which was gifted to Irache in 1109 (Fig. 76). There is nothing exceptional about the traditional octagonal ground plan which follows that of the Jerusalem original, and which has already been seen at Eunate. What is notable is that such round churches in Spain and Southern France display crossed rib-vaulting so placed as to leave a central lantern, clearly derived from Moorish constructional practices.

From Viana onwards lies the contested frontier area between Castile and Navarre known as the Rioja, first held by the Navarrese, who pushed their border beyond Nájera near Burgos, and then incorporated by Alfonso VI into Castile from 1076. The Rioja, fertilized by the head-waters of the Ebro, is a red-flushed, flat plain of vineyards, fruit-trees, wheat and cereals, a vulnerable soft target for ambitious monarchs on either side. For the same reason it had been a cultural focus even before the pilgrimage to Santiago became popular. Before the foundations at Leyre and Irache, the monasteries and hermitages of the Rioja had firmly taken root. It was in these monasteries that the future bridge-builders of the Rioja were to be educated, for example St Dominic of Santo Domingo de la Calzada and his disciple, San Juan de Ortega. Their bridges, built for the pilgrims, stimulated the growth of later settlements in the region. Logroño, on the west side of the Ebro, owed practically everything to the stimulus of the first bridge of twelve arches which was begun in 1080. Earlier, in the tenth century, it had been just a set of farms on a fertile river bank. Like Puente la Reina, it had developed along the standard lines of a town on the route, with an east-west linear pattern and two parallel main streets, characteristically named Rúa Vieja and Rúa Mayor; but unlike Puente la Reina, the river runs parallel to the streets and not at right-angles. From Logroño the pilgrim advances between ploughed fields and vineyards. Ahead to the south-west can be glimpsed the Sierra de la Demanda with its peaks snow-covered for the greater part of the year. This is the north-eastern shoulder of the Guadarrama range and the ragged edge of the Central Meseta or tableland of Old Castile. At the western frontier of Navarre lies Nájera at the end of the fourth stage of the route and another settlement beside a bridge, this time over the River Najerilla, a tributary of the Ebro – not broad, but rapid and violent. Originally of seven arches, the bridge was constructed in the twelfth century by San Juan de Ortega. This settlement was the favourite residence of Sancho the Great of Navarre. Life pivoted round the Monastery of Santa María la Real, the spiritual centre of the region, set back against the strange purple-red rock that angled up behind the town, pocked with holes. Santa María was founded in 1052 by the son of Sancho the Great, García I, alias García Sánchez III of Pamplona/Navarre (1035–54), to shelter the pilgrims. It later became the burial place of the founders and other princes of Navarre, Leon and Castile. The present three-aisled church is a graceful Gothic building of the fifteenth century. The choir-stalls are of the late fifteenth century, with symbols of St James on the backs. But it is the cloisters with their early sixteenth-century filigree stone ornamentation which are the architectural gem of the complex (Fig. 78).

The next significant stopping-point in the fifth stage, which ended in Burgos, the capital of Castile, was Santo Domingo de la Calzada, but many pilgrims took the opportunity of praying first at the shrine of San Millán de la Cogolla, one of the oldest religious houses in the Rioja (Fig. 77). It really consists of two monasteries of different ages, one up amongst the pines and oaks (Monasterio de Suso) and the other below in the often misty and damp Cárdenas valley near the village of Berceo (Monasterio de Yuso). The upper church housed the hermit of San Millán, who lived there for over a hundred years (473–574) and whose magnificent recumbent funerary effigy lies under the rock ledge against which this eleventh-century structure is wedged (Figs. 79, 81). The chapel hollowed out of the rock includes a cube-shaped apse and two aisles divided by three horse-shoe arches. It is stark, mysterious and brooding. Below there

79 *Tombchest of San Millán (detail), Upper Monastery of San Millán de la Cogolla. The cult of San Millán (St Emilion) was widespread through the Rioja and Old Castile, and was in competition with that of St James. Like St James, he appeared on a white horse to defend the Christians in battle against the Moors. This detail of a mourning monk is one of many surrounding the body of the saint, which appears to have been carved out of a single block of alabaster.*

80 (next page) *Pilgrim route leading towards the settlement where St Dominic lived and worked on the roads and bridges, thus giving the town its name, Santo Domingo de la Calzada. In the background the spire of the cathedral breaks the horizon. This feature, uncommon in Spain and usually a sign of foreign influence, was added to the Gothic cathedral in 1762-7 by Martín de Beratúa.*

sprawls a vast and nearly empty monastery and church built over the sixteenth to the eighteenth centuries. It was there, in the thirteenth century, that Master Gonzalo de Berceo wrote a series of local saints' lives and the *Miracles of Our Lady*, whose opening verses were quoted at the beginning of Chapter One.

Those pilgrims who did not digress to San Millán went up the mountainside at the back of Nájera through a gap between the hills, amongst pine groves, vineyards and open country, to Azofra and thence to Santo Domingo de la Calzada on the River Oja, the last tributary of the Ebro to be tackled (Fig. 80). And it flowed through the most contentious piece of territory so far. After the foundation of Burgos, the most direct route to Navarre led through the Montes de Oca, and for a long time the leaders of Castile and Pamplona/Navarre had struggled to establish a frontier somewhere in this hilly, forested region. Pamplona, in the early eleventh century and at the height of its political power, pushed the border as threateningly close as little more than twelve kilometres east of Burgos. During this and the preceding century, troops from both principalities must have fought sorties around the Oja.

One particular young shepherd grew up in this frontier situation. Drawn by the religious life he went to study at a nearby monastery, and then offered himself to San Millán. On being rejected, he decided to live the life of a hermit in a clump of forest on the banks of the Oja a couple of miles south of where pilgrims and other travellers used to ford the river with difficulty. It is recorded that their sufferings inspired him to gather some of the local inhabitants together to construct a more permanent crossing and this led to a settlement growing up which bore his name shortly after his death, Burgo de Santo Domingo. He is credited with having also laid down that part of the pilgrim's road from Nájera to Redecilla. When he died (1109), tradition has it that he was buried on the actual road, and that the new Cathedral was built over his tomb. The church, one of the earliest Gothic constructions in Spain was started in 1158. It belongs mainly to two building periods. The first represents a transition from Romanesque to Gothic style up to 1235; the second occupies the first half of the sixteenth century.

Legends about his miraculous protection of pilgrims after his death continued to circulate throughout western Europe down to the sixteenth century; and in the mid-nineteenth century Robert Southey wrote a poem called the *Pilgrim to Compostella* based on the most famous of all.[3] The legend runs that a young boy accompanied by his parents was passing through the town in the fourteenth century. A serving girl from the inn where the family were staying, consumed by spite because the boy had rejected her, thrust a silver cup in the family baggage and then reported a theft. The boy was arrested as he was leaving and was summarily hanged. The parents continued their pilgrimage in the deepest misery and prayed fervently to St James at Compostela. On the way back they stopped at the gibbet and were

81 *Central nave arcade, Upper Monastery of San Millán de la Cogolla (consecrated 984). This is one of the few surviving pre-Romanesque constructions in Mozarabic style, similar to the lower church in San Juan de la Peña. The monastery was not on the direct pilgrim route, but the cult was sufficiently important for pilgrims to make a detour to the south.*

astounded to hear the corpse speak in joyful tones. Their son said he was indeed alive and that he owed his life to the intervention of the Saint. They rushed back to tell the judge who was sitting down to dinner and he retorted dismissively that the boy was as alive as the cock and hen on the spit in front of him. Whereupon the cock crowed and both birds jumped on the table. For this reason a live cock and hen have been kept in a glass-fronted henhouse in the cathedral transept ever since – much to the distaste of many northern tourists! The shrine over the crypt dates from the early sixteenth century (Fig. 82) and the polychromed statue of the Saint is from the eighteenth century.

The modern division between the province of Burgos and the Rioja falls on the western side of the River Oja, just after the village of Grañón but before the settlers' town of Villafranca de Montes de Oca. This must have remained wild and uncharted territory over centuries, where pilgrims often wandered lost without a guide, living off wild mushrooms and roots or terrified by bandits, until they reached the haven of the Church of San Juan de Ortega, named after the favourite disciple of Santo Domingo and another great builder of bridges.

82 *Shrine of St Dominic (1513), Cathedral of Santo Domingo de la Calzada. The most remarkable section of this Gothic cathedral is the south transept, where the original structure was modified in the early sixteenth century to accommodate a new shrine of the saint. St Dominic is depicted as a pilgrim accompanied by the cock and the hen of the legend (see pp. 88-9).*

III † Through the Tablelands of Castile and Leon

The previous chapter has shown how the frontier between Castile and Navarre shifted east or west according to the political fortunes of either principality. The mountainous region known as the Montes de Oca on the western banks of the River Oja was described in the early vernacular poem about the famous first Count of Castile, Fernán González, as marking the eastern limits of that tiny county, as it then was:

Castile was then a tiny corner,
And the wilds of Oca were the border.[1]

The oak forests on the slopes of the Montes, 1150 metres at their summit were a serious obstacle to the pilgrim after he had crossed the river. The dangers and, at the same time, the hope of divine intervention are expressed in one of the legends contained in the *Liber Sancti Jacobi* in Chapter Three of the second Book. It recalls how a young French pilgrim died there, but was resuscitated and enabled to continue his journey thanks to the protection of St James. After the region's main settlement, Villafranca Montes de Oca, the traveller follows the original road straight over the Sierra, taking at least two hours to reach the next point of call. At Valdefuentes the road divides, the left branch taking the lower and nowadays the modern route to Burgos, while the older follows the traditional track through scrub and forest to the monastery founded by San Juan de Ortega.

The founder of this monastery led a life that gave less to legend than that of his master, Santo Domingo de la Calzada. During the turbulent reign of Alfonso the Battler (1104-34), San Juan visited the Holy Land. After a particularly frightening shipwreck, he made a vow to St Nicholas of Bari to build a church and monastery when he returned home. He chose a spot in the thick scrub of this frontier area to found a community of regular canons of St Augustine with a hospital attached. Apart from this achievement San Juan also contributed to the building and restoration of the stone bridges at Logroño, Nájera, Santo Domingo de la Calzada and laid down the causeway through the marshland on the route to Burgos. His will, preserved in the Church of St Nicholas as a reliquary, refers to the constant threat to the pilgrims of marauding troops or robbers and recalls the building of the monastery (Fig. 87).

The fine apse and crossing are due to his direction as well as some beautifully incised capitals, but the rest of the building is later, including an elaborate Gothic shrine, a gift from Isabel the Catholic (1474-1504), queen of Castile and Leon, who believed that her visit to the Saint's tomb had cured her sterility. The genuine sarcophagus of the Saint has been laid in a modern crypt – rough, primitive and unmarked – beside another elaborately carved one containing an unknown corpse. Close by here lie the monastic buildings which are now in a state of advanced decay, the cloisters strewn with rubble. In the 1940s the village had seventy-three inhabitants; today barely a dozen remain (Fig. 83). However, San Juan de Ortega persists as a focus for modern pilgrims who can find in this isolated place a bed, a roof and shelter by courtesy of a dedicated and hard-working parish priest. From here, rested, they can complete the last few kilometres on the way to Burgos and the end of stage five of the route to Santiago (Fig. 88).

There are two aspects of the history of Burgos which are relevant to us. One relates to the growth of the province, originally the kingdom of Castile, which was to become the most formidable power amongst the Christian kingdoms of the north in the southward drive known as the Reconquest. The other related aspect concerns the development of Burgos as a river-crossing on an important trade-route running from both east to west and north to south, eventually becoming the first major cluster of institutions serving the pilgrim since he crossed the Pyrenees.

The area which lies between the basin of the River Douro and that of the River Tagus contains much of the formative history of Castile. Originally, in the ninth and tenth centuries, the obscure area between the Asturian kingdom (which was based on the city of Leon) and the upper waters of the River Ebro, was just a no-man's land on a vague frontier with no substantial settlements. For that specific reason the Leonese kings afforded the nobility who operated there greater freedom and privileges. These clans or groups were based on fortified strongholds which gave the region its name, and their leaders or counts, appointed by the kings of Leon, exercised this freedom to the full, allying themselves with whatever power, Christian or Moslem, would afford them most advantage; it became difficult to distinguish between the loyal subject and the mercenary for hire. By the late tenth and early eleventh centuries, Fernán González, first Count of Castile, and his household, had become a powerful and semi-independent aristocratic force linked with royal families on either flank. While matters in the province of Galicia to the west engaged the attention of the Leonese, the Navarrese expanded their borders and the overwhelming authority acquired by Sancho the Great of Navarre eventually brought about the establishment of his son, Fernando, as king of a newly created kingdom of Castile. In 1037 Fernando united the two principalities of Leon and Castile under a single king, with Castile as the dominant partner. Under subsequent kings this union prospered, and in particular under Alfonso VI (1072-1109) who moved the

83 (opposite) *One of the few remaining inhabitants of the village of San Juan de Ortega. The fate of this village is similar to many others along the route. Emigration to the towns and cities, a significant trend from the last century, has quickened pace since the 1960s, and many old settlements on the Meseta, the elevated central tableland of Castile and Leon, have become ghost towns.*

Burgos to Rabanal

7 Indicates end of stage in journey
as given by the *Liber Sancti Jacobi*

Scale 1:600000

0   30 km

0   20 mls

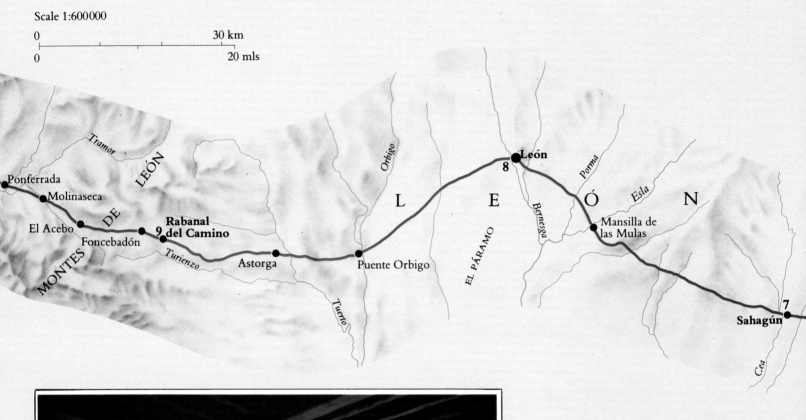

84 *These tastefully restored cloisters of the Nunnery of Las Huelgas, Burgos, are a small masterpiece of Romanesque art, with double columns and rounded arches. They provide a cool refuge from the heat of the Meseta.*

86 *Church of San Martín, Frómista. This church, built in the eleventh and twelfth centuries, is all that remains of the Benedictine monastery that stood on a crossing point of the old pilgrim route with the north-south road from Reinosa in the Cantabrians to the heart of Castile.*

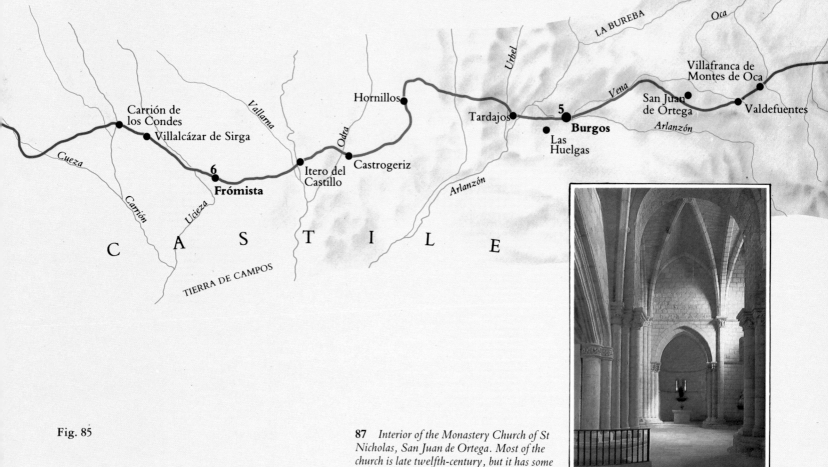

Fig. 85

87 *Interior of the Monastery Church of St Nicholas, San Juan de Ortega. Most of the church is late twelfth-century, but it has some fifteenth-century additions.*

88 *Pilgrim road from San Juan de Ortega to Burgos. Sometimes the route parallels the modern highway, but often it runs along an older road and at times it is only a lane or a barely perceptible track.*

dangerous southern frontier well away from the line of towns developing in the Douro basin, to which he subsequently attracted the monks, merchants and adventurers; and, of course, the pilgrims from the rest of Europe.

Burgos, at first a mere outpost, began in the late ninth century as a settlement on the banks of the River Arlanzón around the castle. It began to expand on the southern slope of the castle hill along a line corresponding to the present Calle de Fernán González. When Castile passed from county to kingdom, Burgos grew rapidly round both sides of the Arlanzón. On either side of the Calle de Fernán González there were shops and hostels; the cathedral lay on the left-hand side and the quarter of St James grew on the slopes up to the castle on the right. At the entrance to the city in the east, the pilgrims arrived first at the Hospital de San Juan, outside the gates, in close proximity to the Church of San Lesmes. Only the cloister and the chapter-house of the monastery remain. The pilgrim then passed through the old city gates, now dismantled, and went down the long Calle de Fernán González to enter the cathedral by the north porch on which one may

89 *Statue of St James as evangelist, carrying the sword of his martyrdom and the Bible, in the north porch of the Cathedral of Santa María, Burgos.*

today still see a somewhat blackened statue of St James as evangelist (Fig. 89). Indeed the original cathedral was dedicated to the Virgin, St James and St Nicholas. Inside this Gothic temple, begun in 1222, the influence of the pilgrimage can be gauged by the prominence of the chapel dedicated to the Saint, the carvings on the choir-seats and in the cloisters (Fig. 91). The rococo altar of the Chapel of Santa Tecla, swirling in gold, green and red, is topped off with an equestrian statue of St James. This chapel has absorbed what had been an older Chapel of St James, entered just beside where the original font of the cathedral is now placed.

90 (next page) *Stubble burning in the fields outside Frómistá at sunset. The wheatlands of the Meseta have for centuries been an aspect of rural life of the region. The Tierra de Campos or Campi Gothici of medieval writers lies at the heart of Castile.*

91,92 *Cathedral of Santa María, Burgos, choir stalls* **(above)** *and corbel of a monk* **(below)**. *The cathedral is an astonishing treasure-house of different styles and details, which the pilgrims would have explored, and still do, in the company of guides.*

The pilgrims left the city by the gate of St Martin, following the line of the river, and eventually came to the most famous hospital of Burgos, the Hospital del Rey founded by Alfonso VIII (1158–1214) expressly for the poor pilgrims. This he placed under the jurisdiction of the famous aristocratic Nunnery of Las Huelgas, so named because it was built upon the meadows where the king took his leisure (Fig. 84). Both still contain reminiscences of the Saint. Las Huelgas has a little chapel with a wooden fourteenth-century statue of St James mounted on the wall; tradition holds that its jointed right arm, holding a sword, was used for dubbing Knights of the Order of St James. The hospital, which is of lavish proportions, lies about a mile away. The deserted ruins that we see today are of much later structures, although the exposed brickwork of the sagging infirmary roof must be of the thirteenth century. Major reforms were carried out in Renaissance times under the Habsburg Emperor Charles V, of which the *Puerta de los Romeros*, the Pilgrim's Gate, is the most memorable, together with the elaborately carved wooden doors of the chapel (Figs. 93, 94).

93,94 *Panels from the mahogany doors, Chapel of the Hospital del Rey, Burgos. In the left-hand panel St Michael and St James, the defenders of the pilgrim way, are represented; between them is a praying figure bearing the cross of Calatrava. The right-hand panel shows three generations of pilgrims. In front, the ailing grandfather, with torn clothes, unshod, leaning on a stick. Father turns his glance to his young son in short trousers, offering him his hand. Behind is the mother, who is breastfeeding on the march. There are three more figures with staffs, two with wide-brimmed straw hats. The Hospital del Rey was founded in the twelfth century and was one of the most important in Spain. The military order of Calatrava provided the first personnel for the hospital.*

The journey to the next place of spiritual significance is a journey into a past which has remained almost unaltered. The pilgrim travels to Sahagún in two stages. According to the Guide these consist of the sixth and the seventh, each approximately fifty-seven kilometres in length; Frómista is the mid-point. We now enter the distinctive Castilian Meseta which comprises high, unending, rolling steppe-like plains where sheep and wheat are sources of wealth. The shepherd treads the routes from winter to summer pasture along the paths cut through the fields of cereal. These plains are spectacularly scenic where the winter lays a tracery of hard frost on the scorched earth; spring transforms them briefly with wild flowers of blues and reds

95 (next page) *A typical Castilian landscape on the Meseta near Castrogeriz. In the past this area was the scene of clashes between Moors and Christians, Castilians and Navarrese. The ruined castle of Castrogeriz on the summit of the hill nearby was already fortified in the ninth century and was a key position in the early years of Castile.*

97 *Nave capital depicting marriage, Church of San Martín de Frómista. The capitals in this church display a series of carvings representing biblical, classical, historical and exemplary tales. The theme of matrimony is dealt with in three characteristic phases, marriage, quarrel and reconciliation. This example represents reconciliation.*

against the evanescent green of the young corn; later the unrelenting summer rolls out a yellow carpet of wheat right up to the limit of the horizon. The sky is for the most part cloudless blue during daylight, pitch-dark at night. Apart from the shallow and seasonal river valleys, water is scarce, and livelihood has been hard for men and animals since the days when the forests were cut away. The low buildings are made of brown adobe held in timber frames, and they seem to crouch against the landscape, indifferent to the passing world. Only those raised by the monks or the nobles are in cut stone.

The road out of Burgos through Tardajos, Hornillos, Hontanas towards Frómista is resolutely flat, and this makes the ruins of the castle on the bare, conical hill of Castrojeriz even more menacing as it scans the plain from east to west. This plain seems to become impossibly wider, with slight undulations, as one crosses the bridge of the River Pisuerga at Itero del Castillo, a bridge of eleven arches which figures in the *Liber Sancti Jacobi*. This river now marks the frontier between the provinces of Burgos and Palencia. In the early Middle Ages it lay across the contested border between Castile and Leon. These lands are known as the Tierra de Campos, the Campos Góticos or the Gothic fields, and refer to the heartland of both kingdoms, used by generations of writers to explain the temperament of the crusading Spaniard (Fig. 95).

96 (opposite) *Entrance arch in mudéjar style leading to the Chapel of St James, Nunnery of Las Huelgas, Burgos. This was a very important and prominent royal nunnery, with many English connections. It was built at the request of King Alfonso VII's wife, Eleanor, daughter of Henry II of England. Edward II stood vigil here and was knighted by Alfonso X, the Wise, in 1254. The Black Prince stayed here in 1367 after the Battle of Navarrete.*

98 *Remains of the eleventh-century Monastery Church of San Benito, Sahagún. This was the first and most important Cluny (Benedictine) foundation in the kingdoms of Leon and Castile. The church plan is very simple, and is attributed to 'Guillelmus maconerius', who had worked on Jaca Cathedral in the early twelfth century.*

99 *There is no change in the landscape as one passes from Castile to Leon. The pilgrim route traverses a frontier on the Meseta which was as disputed in early history as that between Navarre and Castile in the east. Here near Sahagún there are few relieving features. In summer the heat reverberates, and in winter the cold penetrates like a steel blade.*

From the middle of the wheatlands emerges foursquare and solid the only remnant of the Benedictine monastery founded in 1035 by Doña Mayor, the widow of the redoubtable Sancho the Great of Navarre. This remnant is the Church of San Martín de Frómista, dedicated to a French saint amidst the Castilian wheat (Fig. 86). After Jaca, it is one of the earliest Romanesque monuments in the Peninsula, evidence once again of the penetration of masons and clerics along the east–west road. It was, perhaps, over-restored in 1893, to the point where eleven of the capitals are bogus. The false ones, such as one of an old woman cutting bread over a pot to make garlic soup, are marked with an R. The remainder, however, justify the journey (Fig. 97). The image of St James in rosewood in the sanctuary came from a local church. And from the same village came St Elmo, patron saint of sailors and he of St Elmo's fire, a Dominican who looked after Galician seamen at Pontevedra on the Atlantic coast.

Along the road westwards from Frómista are many small hermitages associated with the pilgrimage. Villacázar de la Sirga is of little consequence today, but it was once a town of more than average

101 *Frieze from the central portal, Cathedral of Santa María, Leon. On the left St Michael weighs the souls; those found wanting are delivered up to torment. This cathedral is a splendid example of foreign Gothic in the mature metropolitan French tradition.*

100 (opposite) *Church of Santiago, Carrión de los Condes. The highly sculpted west front is all that is left of this ancient church.*

102 *Pantheon and ceiling fresco of Christ in Majesty and the four evangelists (c.1160), Basilica of San Isidoro, Leon. This impressive pantheon has survived despite the ravages of the centuries and, in particular, the Peninsular War. At the top of the beautifully executed fresco one can just glimpse a fragment of the Nativity.*

103 *North transept (fourteenth-century), Cathedral of Santa María, Leon. Much of the original stained glass has survived, giving a flood of multicoloured light that distinguishes the cathedral of Leon from other Peninsular churches. In all there are 125 windows, 57 roundels and 3 rose windows in the building.*

importance. La Sirga means *calzada* – causeway or metalled road. Besides housing a commandery of the Templars, it possessed a large hospital which backed on to a church dedicated to the Virgin. This Virgin had a miracle-working power which was held to challenge that of St James. According to the story, a rich German merchant, crippled and fallen on evil times, sought relief by going to Santiago. Not only was he not cured but he went blind and was abandoned by his companions. This Virgin listened to his call and restored him to health and wealth. Many of these legends were turned into poetry by the scholar-king Alfonso X of Castile and Leon (1252-84) in his *Cantigas de Santa María*. Hundreds of miracles of this type along the road proclaim the greater virtues of the local saint, but for the modern reader or traveller this practice can only confirm the all-pervasive influence of St James. The church itself at Villacázar is Transitional; the walls and narrow windows are still Romanesque but the Gothic pointed arch timidly appears. The impressive southern porch, stretching up the full height of the wall, is overlaid with lines of stone figures from the Bible and past history. Inside, in the Chapel of St James at the end of the south transept lie the elaborately wrought tombs of the Infante Felipe, fifth son of St Ferdinand of Castile (1217/30-1252) and his wife, Leonor Ruiz de Castro.

By far the most important settlement traversed by the pilgrims in the Tierra de Campos was Carrión de los Condes. Situated on the left bank of the River Carrión, on a slight elevation over the River (a significant advantage in this sort of landscape), the town was a defensive key along the Leonese frontier and the seat of the 'warrior' Counts of Carrión. This accounts for the name of the locality which had been known as Santa María del Carrión, the name in fact of its principal church, Santa María del Camino, under whose massive porch the pilgrims sheltered while listening to the stories connected with the mysterious stone sculptures which line its façade. Further along, on the Plaza Mayor and at the corner of a street characteristically named la Rúa, stands the façade of the Church of Santiago (Fig. 100). It is all that is left of a Romanesque structure burnt centuries later in the Peninsular War (1808-13). It presents an impressive façade with a carved display of the twenty-four Elders of the Apocalypse, and many other scenes. On the western side of the town, past the bridge over the river, is the Benedictine Monastery of San Zoilo, with its well-known pilgrims' hostel. It was founded by one of the counts in the eleventh century on receipt of the remains of the Saint sent from Cordoba by their son Fernand. Unfortunately only a few fragments are left of this important monastery. The bulk of the present building dates from the Renaissance, or later.

The town of Sahagún is still encompassed by the rolling landscape and is built of brick. Its past is inseparable from the story of the monastery (Fig. 98). This foundation, dedicated to the martyrs St Facundus and St Primitivus, who are almost unknown outside Spain, was already in existence by 904, long before Alfonso VI asked Abbot

104 (opposite) *Cloisters, Cathedral of Santa María, Leon. The cloister walls were built before 1458, but the vaulting is much later (c.1538-40). Faint frescoes by Nicolás Francés have survived. In the forefront is a pinnacle that comes from another part of the cathedral.*

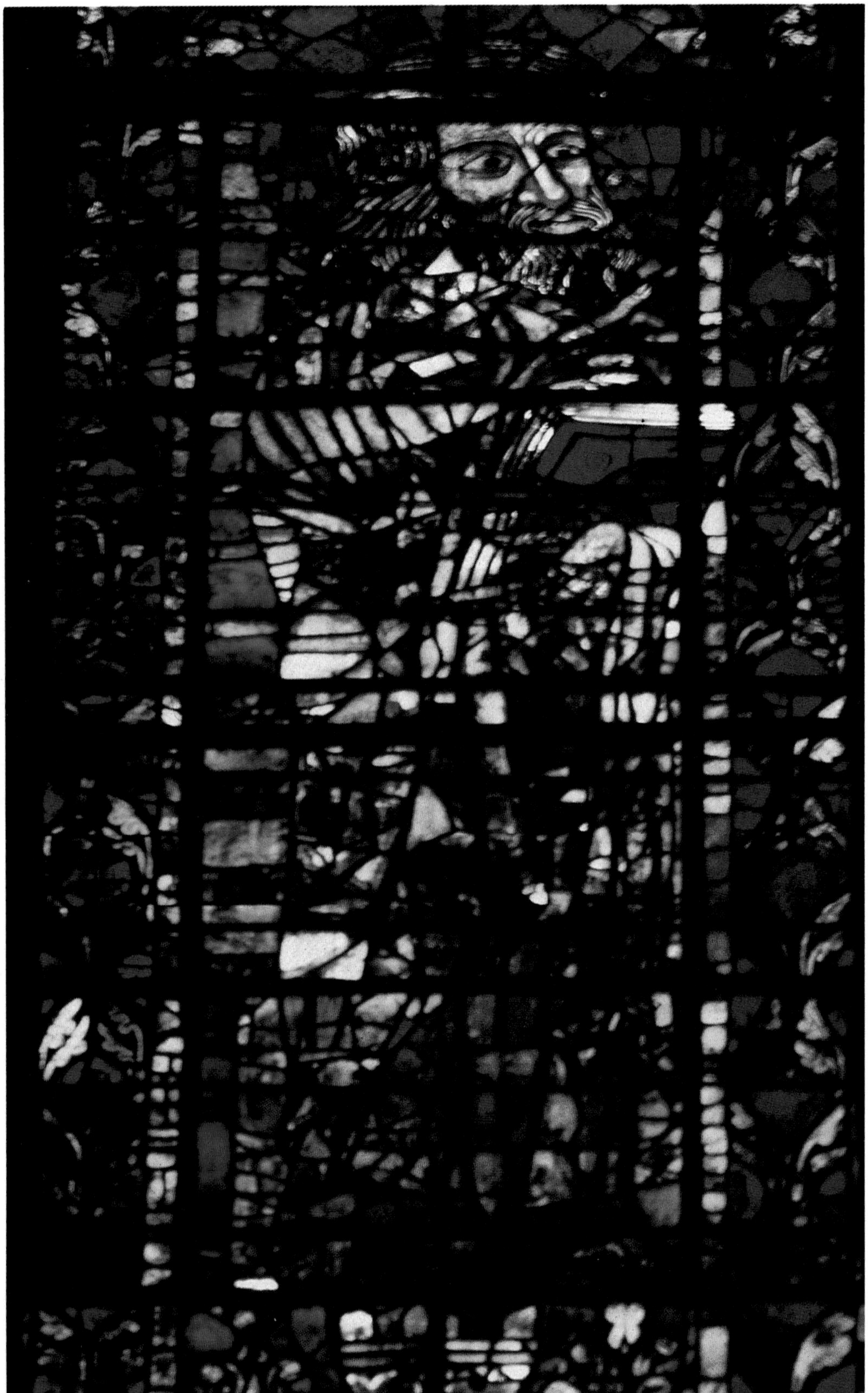

106 *Parish Church of Santa María, Rabanal del Camino. This church was built in the twelfth and thirteenth centuries, and may at one time have belonged to the Knights Templar, a military order founded in the early twelfth century, whose profession it was to guard the pilgrimage routes.*

105 *Stained-glass figure of St James as an evangelist in the clerestory of the Cathedral of Santa María, Leon. There is another window of the saint in the Chapel of St James.*

Hugh of Cluny during a short interview in Burgos to send his monks there. They arrived in 1079; and as a famous Archbishop of Toledo said two centuries later, 'As Cluny excels in France, so this monastery stands over all those of its order in Spain.'[2] Favoured by the Crown, it expanded rapidly in wealth and possessions, and many of its monks became bishops. It also had a hospital with seventy beds which functioned up to the seventeenth century. However, of this great brick and stone edifice, only an arch and a tower remain; rather like Cluny itself. Of the other nine brick churches, only four survive. Outside the town, on the shoulder of a low rise on the south side, can be seen the outline of the Franciscan monastery whose Virgin was known as la Peregrina, and whose sacristy still preserves enchanting coloured stucco-work of Moorish inspiration.

Sahagún was a rich town partly because of the abbey, but also due to the persistent influx of merchants and craftsmen encouraged by the Crown. This is the anonymous chronicle of Sahagún:

Accordingly, inasmuch as the said king Alfonso VI had ordered that there should be a town there, burgesses of many and various kinds and trades came from all parts of the world – smiths, carpenters, tailors, furriers and shoe-makers. These men also included many from foreign provinces and kingdoms – Gascons, Bretons, Germans, English, Burgundians, Normans, Toulousians, Provençals, Lombards and many other merchants of divers nations and strange languages. And thus he populated and created a considerably sized town.

But there was trouble between the all-powerful abbots and the frustrated traders which broke out into open violence. The king had to make the peace, and with peace came prosperity.

And because the merchants and burgesses of Sahagún disposed of their merchandise peacefully and traded without fear, they came and brought goods from all parts, such as gold and silver and every kind of fashion of clothes. Thus the townsmen and inhabitants became very rich and well supplied with many delightful things.[3]

However, they never wrested power from the monks. When the abbey died at the end of the Middle Ages, the town shrank. Furthermore, when one leaves Sahagún, the epic dimension of Castile is left behind. Sahagún is the last town which has been connected with the memories of Charlemagne, Roland, and the martyred soldiers who died for the recovery of Spain from the Moors. Indeed there is very little legend recorded in the *Liber Sancti Jacobi* about the remainder of the journey until one arrives in Santiago itself.

Sahagún to Leon was the eighth stage in the route, approximately fifty-two kilometres in length. It passed through an area of deprivation where it was necessary to sleep on the ground or under straw roofs (Fig. 99). Laffi, a seventeenth-century traveller, reported having seen the wolves eating the corpse of a pilgrim.[4] The past is very present. Mansilla de las Mulas has not lost all its walls and gates; one can

107 *The Puente de Orbigo on the route between Leon and Astorga was built in the thirteenth to fifteenth centuries and has more than twenty arches. The greater part of the medieval stonework has been preserved. In 1434 this was the setting for the famous joust of Suero de Quiñones (see p. 119).*

clearly guess at the medieval structure of a frontier town set on the banks of the River Esla. North of the town can still be seen the bases of the arches of the Roman bridge that carried the road on towards Leon. Leon was a recognized Roman settlement owing its name to the Seventh Legion, but it is doubtful if much survived from that age up to the repopulation of the region in the late ninth century. Its princes can hardly have had much experience of urban life and organization before the tenth century; Oviedo and Pamplona would have been the closest examples available to them, and the former was probably little more than a fortified palace. But in the tenth and eleventh centuries, partly due to the influx of Christians from the Moorish south, and also because of the expansion of the trade-routes, much was learned from the experience of town life under Islam, and from that of the immigrant Franks in general.

Leon's period of authority comes before the rise of Castile. Alfonso III (866-910) launched a programme of building that echoes the splendour of Charlemagne's reign in a Spanish setting. Alfonso's interest in Santiago and the cult of St James was paramount in the early development of the pilgrimage, as we shall see later. Ordoño II (914-24), his successor, proclaimed Leon as the capital of his kingdom and in his time it became the most important city in Christian Spain. No urban settlement had so many churches and monasteries, and it was not eclipsed by Burgos until late in the eleventh century. One of the main foundations which afforded Leon its spiritual authority was the basilica built in 1063 to accommodate with dignity the bones of St Isidore, the greatest scholar in the West (*c*.560-636). The transfer of these relics from Seville to a Christian burial ground was the occasion of great ceremony, and in the same year the body of St Vincent was brought from Avila to the Church of San Juan. The authorities in Leon were clearly intent on making it a centre not only of spiritual reverence but also of scholarship and, most significantly, of royal power. In the late eleventh century a royal mausoleum was constructed as a disproportionately large portico to the basilica. The edifice embraces three naves and six cupolas covered with a set of frescos which may be dated about 1160 (Fig. 102). These are exceptional for the quality of the paint and the clarity of tone in colours of ochre, violet, blue and yellow.

The pilgrim route through the city was a prominent feature. Fernando II of Leon (1157-80) went so far as to change its path in 1168 so that it should not run as before down the present Avenida del Generalísimo, but along the present Calle del Cid, past San Isidoro and thence out through a special gate, Renueva, which he had opened in the walls. Along this route the pilgrims would have visited the elegant Gothic cathedral, originally built on the site of the Palace of Ordoño II. It had suffered from invasions, reconstructions and demolitions until the present edifice emerged between 1255 and the end of the same century (Figs. 101, 104). Its appeal does not reside in its exterior; it is within that all its glories are contained. Neither large nor tall by French standards, it possesses an unmatched grace in the way in which the stone barely contains the vivid stained-glass expanse which occupies almost all of the wall surface (Figs. 103, 105). Although dedicated to the Virgin, the cathedral has always carried images of St James. On the left side of the façade, a couple of metres from the ground, stands a statue whose supporting column is heavily scored with striations probably made by pilgrims with metal objects, such as medals or crosses. The Saint is represented on the main altar and in the stained glass of the clerestory, and also in the tall sixteenth-century window in the Chapel of St James.

Scattered about the city were about seventeen hospitals and hostels of which the most important was that of San Marcos. This was begun in the mid-twelfth century, together with its chapel. The hospital still stands to the east of the present church in melancholy anonymity. The Church of St James could not be more obvious with its profuse decorative relief of scallop-shells, while the cloister houses a collection of sculptures and statues from the Road. There is an equestrian figure of St James in this church (Fig. 4), as well as in a medallion over the main portal of the imposing Renaissance monastery, which was constructed in 1513, and is also lavishly garnished with scallop-shells, busts of kings and queens, priors and warriors. It was built for the Knights of the Order of St James and is today a state-run hotel, the second such conversion along the road.

From San Marcos the pilgrims crossed the River Bernesga and began the last trek across the Meseta, following the ancient Roman road to Asturica, or modern Astorga. Stage nine of the journey, some sixty-four kilometres in length, ends in the ascent of the mountain ranges that separate Leon from Galicia. To the north, the Cantabrian mountains become more prominent, particularly Peña Ubiña, which is nearly always covered in snow. In the vicinity of the city of Leon the aridity has been softened by market-gardening and irrigation, drawn from the River Orbigo. Over the Orbigo river-bed, and the slopes that incline towards it, the medieval bridge spins out its twenty arches; only the four great pointed arches at the centre are ancient. On the western side the Knights of St John founded a hospital of which little remains, only in the name of the village, Hospital de Orbigo, and a few fragments on the west side of the Plaza Mayor. In the Jubilee Year of 1434 when St James's Day fell on a Sunday, a Leonese knight named Suero de Quiñones handed a document to a herald. The herald then read out loud that the knight, being in thrall to a lady in whose honour he wore an iron collar, would challenge anyone who passed the bridge with his band of nine men. Near the bridge a great wooden enclosure was built, where Suero and his knights fought sixty-eight French, German, Italian, Portuguese and Castilian champions (Fig. 107). All those who were genuinely on pilgrimage in that jubilee year were allowed to pass unchallenged and unharmed. Afterwards Suero and his band went to Compostela where he offered to St James a golden bracelet, which is on exhibit to this day in the reliquary chapel. All these events were dutifully recorded by a scribe whose account of the medieval joust became so popular that manuscript copies circulated throughout Europe, were translated and later passed into print.[5]

On their way towards the mountains the pilgrims entered the walled city of Astorga by the eastern gate, the Puerta Sol – now demolished. Embattled Astorga is like an elongated rectangle balanced from east to west on a stretch of raised terrain. Once inside, the pilgrims continued up the Rúa de las Tiendas (now the Calle San Francisco) to the Plaza Mayor. From there to the cathedral ran the Rúa Nova (now Calle Pío Guillén), past the Calle de Santiago and then on to the right of the church. Beside the west end was situated the Hospital de San Juan. Little remains of the original building (part of which is now a museum), where tradition says that St Francis stopped on his way through to Santiago. This city, connected with the precious-metal trade from Roman times, had a disproportionately large number of hostels and hospitals – twenty-two against thirty or so in Burgos – one of which was founded in honour of the martyr Thomas à Becket by a personal friend of his. Perhaps this was because of the need to gather strength in this 'strange and lonely city, facing westwards towards the heaped ranges of mountains which divide Spain from Galicia', as George Borrow put it in the *Bible in Spain*.[6]

Rabanal del Camino, the end of stage nine of the Guide, and at the foot of the range, takes the traveller right back into a lost rural past. It is a village of cobbled streets and hard-packed soil with drainage down the centre, rough rubble walls and roofs thatched with straw or broom, some of which have collapsed on wretched broken beams. It is the colour of slate set in a sombre, rough landscape of pasture and heather, with little arable land. There was a Templar house here in the twelfth century, perhaps backing on to the angular Romanesque parish church (Fig. 106) from whose primitive bell-tower one can get a first clear view of the Montes de León, and in particular Monte Irago, with the abandoned village of Foncebadón on the eastern slopes. From here one can also look back at the plain in which Astorga lies, and watch the heavens at day's end. Here it is common to witness spectacular sunsets when the sky is spread with radiating bars of deep reds and purples against a background of watered greens and blues, quickly to be extinguished by the thick blackness of the nights. At the summit of the pass, 1490 metres high, the Cruz de Ferro juts into the sky – a pile of loose stones holding a long wooden stake with an iron cross on top. Every single stone there was left by Galician peasants on their seasonal trips to Castile for the harvesting.

IV † Beyond the Mountains to the Shrine

From the pass of Foncebadón the road twists and plunges downwards on the tenth stage through occasional slate-built villages into the wooded bowl of the valley known as El Bierzo, a sort of ante-chamber to Galicia. The population on the slopes is scattered and thin, especially in the higher reaches. In order to discourage emigration, and to help the travellers, the inhabitants of El Acebo, one of the first villages one comes across on the reverse slope, were freed of all taxes as long as they placed a line of stakes before the snow fell to show the pilgrims and travellers where the hidden road lay (Fig. 113). But El Bierzo has not been able to resist the penetration of industrialization. The inner-eye, attuned to the past, suffers an unexpected jolt at the sight of the first major town on the valley bottom, Ponferrada.

The intrusion of the modern world takes the form of an untidy welter of workers' flats; high-tension cables, smelting plants and low-level smog, which is only partially compensated for by the sight of a restored Templar castle near the river-crossing with its so-called iron bridge, *Pons Ferrata*, which gave its name to the medieval settlement. About fifty kilometres later, one comes to the end of stage ten in the largest town of this, for the most part, undisturbed and rural sequence of steep valleys plentifully watered by fresh, clear streams full of fish, and covered with fruit trees, vines, almonds, olives, groves of oak and sweet chestnut.

The pilgrims would enter Villafranca del Bierzo near the Church of St James. It rests unpretentiously on a cobbled rise opposite the decaying Palace of the Condes de Villafranca with huge pepper-pot towers at each corner and conical slate roofs. This modest church has a single nave and a *Puerta del Perdón* on the north side. Local legend has it that if a pilgrim for good reason could not carry on to Santiago, he could pray to be excused here from further journeying without renouncing the benefits of his pilgrimage.

As the name of the town suggests, it was settled by foreign immigrants (Franks) from the eleventh century onwards, including both merchants and monks. The Friars' Church displays a beautiful *mudéjar artesonado* or decorated timber roof. The early pilgrims fill their reports with praises of El Bierzo, and the *Liber Sancti Jacobi* adds that on leaving the borders of Leon and the mountains behind, one was

108 *Sunset over a bleak, uninhabited mountain landscape, seen from the pass at Foncebadón.*

110 *On the lower reaches of Monte Irago there are a few cultivated patches where fodder is grown for the sheep and goats that subsist in this region.*

To Santiago

111 *The distant peaks of the Sierra de Telemo, rising to over 2,000 metres, viewed from the flank of Monte Irago near the tiny village of Foncebadón.*

11 Indicates end of stage in journey as given by the *Liber Sancti Jacobi*

Scale 1:600000

0   30 km

0   20 mls   **Fig. 109**

VALLE DE SARRIA

Sarria

11 Triacastela

Samos

Barbadelo

Cebrero

SIERRA DEL CAUREL

EL BIERZO

Villafranca del Bierzo **10**

Cua

Burbia

Ponferrada

Molinaseca

Tramor

DE LEÓN

Rabanal 9 del Camino

El Acebo

Foncebadón

MONTES

Turienzo

Astorga

Tuerto

Puente Orbigo

now virtually in Galician territory with plenty of white bread, cider, milk and honey, gold and silver. This was a land of contrasts, of rich valleys surrounded by high mountains, and it must have seemed like a green paradise after the sombre rigours of the Central Meseta. It appeared like that even in its savage state, before the pilgrim route was heavily travelled, when the region was sought by hermits and small communities of monks. More than twenty monasteries are known to have been founded here, many before the tenth century. Thus a network of paths and tracks existed from early times, worn through the undergrowth by pilgrims in search of holy men. Long before the Moorish invasion, they had established a local ascetic tradition and a written rule in refuges remote from traders and explorers. Even the Romans had only partially penetrated the region, which was ultimately named after one of their small outposts, Bergidum Flavium.

The last pass, leading out of El Bierzo into the coastal plain of Galicia, was probably the most difficult of all for the pilgrim (Fig. 114).[1] There is a certain divine logic that the drama of the journey should reach a point of rest before the final physical test. Afterwards it would literally be downhill all the way. Cebrero, or Cebreiro in the Galician dialect which is now used by officialdom on a par with Castilian, was one of the dry passes of the road. It stands at 1293 metres and is probably not far from a Roman road, which would have been later replaced by a medieval track. There used to be a monastery and hospital nearby, round which a little settlement grew up, built out of the local slatey slabs. Prudent scholars tend to think of the earliest foundations as dating from the late eleventh century; by the sixteenth century the monastery had been reduced to four monks and the church had fallen into disrepair.

Today the village of about some fifty inhabitants is a dour, bleak archaism with what the romantic would classify as Celtic charm. The church has been restored and still has its twelfth-century Madonna. A simple but comfortable hostel is run by the local priest and frequented at intervals by mining experts boring for zinc and lead. But the pilgrim can sleep for free in the strange, circular, stone structures thatched with a wigwam-like roof of broom. Local interest has preserved these vestiges of a prehistoric past, of which there are only a few left in Galicia and Asturias. They are called *pallozas*, and consist of a circle of dry-stone walling up to shoulder height with a central support that holds up the roof. The windows are tiny and the low doors are framed in massive stone lintels of granite.

From the heights of Cebrero the road descends, circling and doubling back on itself through sweeps of gorse and broom. Here and there one can glimpse stretches of the original road surface covered with small blocks of quartz. Eventually the village of Triacastela appears at the foot, the end of the eleventh stage which began in the preceding valley at Villafranca. There are not many large foundations on this section of the road, but one that must be mentioned is the Monastery of San Julián de Samos, set in an isolated valley on a bend

112,113 *The descent from Foncebadón into El Bierzo takes the traveller through landscape such as this* **(above)** *in the vicinity of El Poyo to villages such as Acebo* **(above right)**. *This is a view of the main street. The dwellings are constructed of rubble, mostly of a slatey stone, with* *wooden balconies and living quarters on the first floor and animals on the ground floor. The ox-cart is still a common means of transport. It is the responsibility of the inhabitants to maintain the surface of the road in their villages, hence its often poor condition.*

of the river between two mountains. As the pilgrims descended they could see its domes project above the trees. This is one of the most ancient and celebrated monasteries in Galicia. Between the eighth and tenth centuries it became a refuge for monks from the Moorish south. None of this survives today due to a disastrous fire in the 1950s, but the abbey in its modern form still offers shelter to the passing pilgrim (Fig. 121).

From here on the countryside has no significant features of interest, except perhaps at Portomarín where the medieval town was submerged under a reservoir in the 1920s and the Commandery Church of the Hospitallers re-erected stiffly in a newly-arcaded Plaza Mayor. The new village produces a somewhat stagey effect. Portomarín was an important locality in Roman times with its bridge over the River Miño, and in the medieval period it was the duty of the Commandery to look after the hospital, a stretch of the road and the

114 (next page) *View of the mountains from the pass at Cebrero, altitude c.1,300 metres. The pilgrim who has just been roasted on the plains is now exposed to the icy winds that sweep down from the mountains of Leon.*

115 *Stone bridge over the River Meruelo, leading to the main street of the village of Molinaseca, at the western foot of the Foncebadón pass. The bridge, built in the twelfth and thirteenth centuries, has been much restored.*

bridge, which has been renewed many times to the present day. However, the major military order operating here and in other frontier areas was the Order of the Knights of St James. The Order came into being on the southern frontier, when Fernando II of Leon (1157–88) conquered Cáceres and entrusted its defence to a brotherhood of Christian knights. From these small beginnings the Order grew until its possessions covered large areas of north-western, central and southern areas of the Peninsula. One of its monastery churches lies not far to the west of Portomarín at Vilar de Donas, which was a chapterhouse and a cemetery for the Galician region (Fig. 119). The dank, lichen-covered granite nave is scattered with sarcophagi of knights who had fought to clear the area of bandits and armed gangs, for Galicia, like the Basque region, was prone to violent and bloody feuds.

At Palas do Rey the twelfth stage of the journey concludes and the thirteenth and last begins. Each of the little villages on the now gently descending road contains some fragment of interest, like that of Leboreiro, known in ancient and modern times for its hares, where they are restoring the paved pilgrim road through the Calle Mayor

(Fig. 122), or Mellid, in whose parish church there is a charming fresco of trumpet-playing angels, or Arzúa which has a rough but aggressively-painted wooden statue of St James on horseback with a bent sword and a dusty tricorne hat (Fig. 124). The road now runs through patches of scrubland on red earth, recently planted with pines and eucalyptus and strewn with the usual detritus that heralds the approach of a large city. One final ceremony remains for the pilgrim to complete before he prepares for entry. Some five kilometres from Compostela, there rises on the south side of the village of San Marcos a low scrub-covered hill called Monxoi or the 'hill of jubilation' from whence the pilgrim could have his first glimpse of the towers of the cathedral.

The remaining few kilometres to the walled city would have been an occasion of tearful rejoicing after more than seven-hundred kilometres of the road from the Pyrenees. Those who had come on horseback normally dismounted in respectful humility. The vast majority of pilgrims made the entry to Compostela from the north-east, passed the leper hospital, crossed the River Sar, traversed a small grove of

116 *Parish Church at Corullón, near Villafranca del Bierzo. This typical single-nave Romanesque structure lies about six kilometres south of the pilgrim route. It has a magnificent south door, surmounted by three bays of blind arcading. Many little churches like this are tucked into the valley folds.*

117,118 *Sunset landscape* **(above)** *and* **(right)** *autumn mist and trees, seen from the mountain pass at Cebrero. This area is practically devoid of population and cultivation; the ground is covered with rough grass, sedge and broom.*

119 *Knight's tomb from the twelfth-century Church of the Knights of the Order of St James, Vilar de Donas. At one time the order had a monastery on this site.*

trees, climbed a low hill and entered by the Porta Francigena, or Puerta del Camino, one of the seven entrances. Then they took the Via Francigena, the only major east–west street, climbed the rise up the Calle Casas Reales to the modern Plaza de Cervantes, then down the Azabachería to the Plaza de la Inmaculada and on to the open area known as 'Paradise' on the north side of the cathedral. Along these streets were lined the traders, the money-changers, the makers of jet objects, the sellers of trinkets and some of the many hospitals. Aimery Picaud, writing in the *Liber Sancti Jacobi* in Chapter Nine of the Fifth Book, can provide the best guide to a past which has almost disappeared today:

SANTIAGO DE COMPOSTELA
THE MEDIEVAL CITY

1 Puerta del Camino (Porta Francigena)
2 Puerta de San Roque (opened 16th cent.)
3 Puerta de la Peña (Porta Penne)
4 Puerta de San Martín (Porta de Subfratribus)
5 Puerta de la Trinidad (Porta de Sancto Peregrino)
6 Puerta de Fajeira (Porta da Felgariis)
7 Puerta de Mazarelas (Porta de Macerellis)
8 Puerta de la Mámoa (Porta de Susannis)
9 Hospital of St Felix
10 Old Hospital
11 Hospital of Calle de Carnicerías Viejas
12 Monastery and hospital of San Payo
13 Hospital de Jerusalén
14 Hospital of Calle de Santa Cristina
15 Hospital founded by Sarracino González
16 Hospital de Nuestra Señora del Camino
17 Hospital de Santa Ana
18 Hospital de la Reina
19 Hospital de Salomé
20 Hospital de San Juan
21 Hospital de San Roque
22 Hospital de Carretas
23 Hospital de los Reyes Católicos
24 Cathedral (see inset)
25 San Martin Pinario
26 College of St Jerome
27 College of Fonseca
28 College of Nuestra Señora de los Remedios
29 University
30 Convent of Nuestra Señora de la Cerca
31 San Miguel de los Agros
32 Formerly Iglesia de la Trinidad
33 Plaza del Campo (de Cervantes)
34 Santa María Salomé
35 Convent of San Francisco
36 Capilla de las Ánimas
37 Palace of Archbishop Gelmírez
38 Market Square de las Platerías
39 Plaza del Obradoiro
40 Palacio de Rajoy (Town Hall)
41 Formerly 'Paradise' Square
42 Calle Azabachería
43 Via Francigena

The Cathedral

A Steps
B Pórtico de la Gloria
C Nave
D North Portal
E South Portal
F Sanctuary/altar

Fig. 120

122 *The village of Leboreiro, west of Palas do Rey, has a little Romanesque church and an ancient pilgrims' hospital. Here some of the villagers are re-laying the main street, which leads towards Santiago.*

121 (previous page) *The Benedictine Monastery of San Julián de Samos on the pilgrim road through El Bierzo. Documents speak of a monastic foundation here as far back as the eighth century. Of these foundations, nothing remains, and there is little left of the subsequent Romanesque structure. The present monastery has been largely constructed since 1951, when a fire destroyed most of the earlier buildings. It still welcomes pilgrims.*

When we French want to enter the Basilica of the Apostle, we go in on the north side. In front of the portal and by the roadside is the Hospital of St James for poor pilgrims, and beyond there is the 'Paradise' down a flight of nine stairs. At the foot is set a marvel of a fountain which has no equal in the rest of the world. This fountain rests on three stone steps which bear a beautiful concave stone basin, a deeply carved dish, so big I think fifteen men could bathe in it easily…Beyond the fountain lies 'Paradise', paved with stone, where the pilgrims buy scallop-shells, the sign of St James, wineskins, shoes, pouches of deerskin, purses, thongs, belts and all manner of medicinal herbs and much more besides…'Paradise' is as big as a stone's throw in either direction.

Aimery goes on to describe the north and south portals, and finally the main or western entrance. But what he described is not what we see today, particularly the famous Pórtico de la Gloria carved by Master Mateo between 1168 and 1188 (Figs. 123, 125, 130). One struggles with words to capture the impact of this representation of the Majestic Transfiguration of Our Lord, flanked by the Tetramorph and surrounded by the whole orchestra of twenty-four Elders, with their minutely-worked musical instruments, and conversing in pairs. Below

123 *The apostle Luke writing his gospel on the bull, his symbolic animal, central tympanum, Pórtico de la Gloria (1168-88), Cathedral of Santiago de Compostela.*

the lintel, framing the central portal are Moses with the tablets on the left and Peter with the keys on the right. Backed against the upper half of the central column, taking as it were with ease the weight of the tympanum, is a seated St James in benevolent repose, the head with its encrusted halo inclined towards the penitent. Below him, in fashioned marble set against the granite column, stretches Christ's genealogy, while the column head represents the Trinity; its base is a bearded sphinx. On either side of the doorway stand the prophets to the left and the apostles to the right, supported on colonnades (Fig. 128). This central porch evokes harmony and peace, not only in its general composition, but in the detail of Moses's grandeur or the beardless youth of Daniel. The division of the elect from the damned has been pushed to the entrances at either side of the central door, so that the air of contained joyfulness is not disturbed by ecstasy or anguish.

Santiago de Compostela is a typical 'pilgrimage church', grand in scale. While Ste Foy at Conques has the most picturesque situation, Santiago is without doubt the most commanding. Like other pilgrimage churches it was built in granite, fortified and has remarkable sculptural decoration; but only Santiago had the richness of sculpture on all three entrances and a complete set of aisles and galleries which encompass the whole structure. And only Santiago was planned for the complete set of nine towers, the ideal of Charlemagne's time.[2] None of the towers were ever properly finished, for this splendid old cathedral was not completed until the late eighteenth century, and its exterior features are masked under the Baroque style.

The great western portals are enclosed in a narthex or porch at the top of a set of Renaissance steps. But once the pilgrim passes the threshold, the Romanesque style predominates and he is afforded a completely free view of the majestic sweep of the central nave under the continuous barrel-vault of stone. This leads the eye to the main altar, the focus of special devotion over the centuries. The altar today is Baroque (1658-77) and the sanctuary early eighteenth century. Behind stands the raised alcove where the seated, multicoloured, stone figure of St James is worshipped (Fig. 133). The modern pilgrim ascends a few steps on a stone stair at the side of the altar, finds himself on a level with the back of the Saint's image, embraces him with both arms and descends on the other side. He may also go down into the crypt where the 'remains' of the Saint's body were rediscovered in 1879, authenticated by the Pope and replaced in a silver urn.

The original altars of the cathedral were dedicated in 1105 and the final consecration came a century later in 1211, not long after the Pórtico de la Gloria was finished. Up to the early years of the twelfth century the pilgrims could venerate directly the tomb of St James. At some later, unspecified date, it was put away under the main altar. According to Aimery, no one had dared to change this altar which he had measured with his own hand as five palms high, twelve long and seven wide. It was of gold and silver and represented the Lord enthroned with the twenty-four Elders. Over this was a canopy resting

124 (opposite) *Wooden statue of St James the Moorslayer, Parish Church of Santiago, Arzúa. This rather dusty and decrepit statue was once used regularly in processions, but today it is tucked away in a corner. It is a piece of folk carving, probably nineteenth-century.*

125 *The apostles Peter, Paul, James the Lesser and John, Pórtico de la Gloria, Cathedral of Santiago de Compostela. An inscription on the lintel of the west portal records that the sculpture was executed by Matthew (Mateo) master mason. He had been commissioned to do the work by King Fernando II in 1168.*

on four columns painted inside and out with angels, Old Testament figures and apostles. Behind this altar, one supposes, was placed the stone-carved figure of St James, often repainted.

Generations of local authorities, secular and spiritual, have managed to preserve the commanding situation of the cathedral on the western side. The façade was erected on an undercroft or crypt, which entailed the erection of a set of approaching steps. It is flanked and faced by low buildings which surround an ample flagged square known as the Plaza do Obradoiro. To the left stands the hospital of the early sixteenth century, built on the orders of the Catholic king and queen Fernando and Isabel, the largest medieval hospital in Spain, with four magnificent courtyards. On the right is the College of St Jerome, now the University Rectory; in front, the imposing Renaissance Palacio de Rajoy, now the Town Hall. Most of the prominent buildings in the vicinity are due, directly or indirectly, to the energy and political acumen of the three Fonseca Archbishops of Santiago, whose authority was supreme from the mid-fifteenth to mid-sixteenth century. The *studium generale* or fore-runner of the university was

126,127 *Two fragments on south porch, Cathedral of Santiago de Compostela. The south porch, known as Puerta de las Platerías (the silversmiths' door), is no longer as it was described in Aimery Picaud's Guide. The pieces have been jumbled about, and probably other pieces have been added, such as this St David* **(left)**, *playing his rebec and seated in cross-legged fashion, and the seated saint* **(right)**. *The Plaza de las Platerías to the west of the porch once housed the workshops of the silversmiths.*

128 *The prophet Isaiah with a scroll (right) and Moses with the tablets of the law (far right), central portal, Cathedral of Santiago de Compostela. The prophets stand on the left side of the porch, the apostles on the right.*

started during their period of office and the Colegio de Fonseca was built by Fonseca III as a near twin to the one he had founded in Salamanca. These granite buildings, the arcaded, narrow streets, the cathedral, and students and pilgrims combine to give the city its special sort of magic. Those who come in the summer to write of Santiago describe it as a sleepy town, rather like Scotland on a Sunday! They have not been there during university term when half the population is under twenty and not given to silence. But why, one may ask, did it all come about in this particular place?

St James in his missionary days is credited with having landed in southern Spain and journeyed through Mérida to Padrón and Iria Flavia, the former a fishing village on the River Sar in Galicia near the Atlantic coast. He is said to have founded the bishoprics of Braga in north Portugal, Lugo in Galicia and Astorga in Leon. Then he experienced the miraculous vision on the banks of the River Ebro, when the Virgin Mary instructed him to build a church at a spot where her angels had placed a pillar; this is now the Cathedral of Nuestra Señora del Pilar in Saragossa. But James is not credited with great success over conversions, particularly in Galicia. Disappointed, he returned to Jerusalem, and the famous medieval collection of saints' lives, the *Golden Legend*, widely publicized his sufferings there. According to this account, he met two magicians, Hermogenes and Philetus, who with their arts had managed to steal away those who had once listened to the word of Christ. They set their demons on James, but the devils found they could not touch him and ultimately as a result of this the two magicians were converted. King Herod, encouraged by the Jews, condemned James to death. On the way to his execution, James cured a paralytic and converted the scribe who accompanied him, and both were beheaded at the same time. The Jews' hatred was so pronounced that they left the head and body unburied to be eaten by dogs and other wild animals. But James's disciples collected their master's body and took it to the seashore. A magic boat of stone appeared with no crew; they got into this and it swept out to sea with the precious corpse. In seven days this miraculous boat bore them to the village of Padrón. There they got out and tethered the boat (Fig. 129).[3] Suddenly the body soared up to the level of the sun and was pursued by the disciples for about twenty kilometres to the east where it came to earth in the kingdom of a powerful pagan queen, Lupa. She hated Christians and adored graven idols. It was obvious that she had not heard of St James on his previous mission. The disciples asked her if they could bury the corpse nearby. She sent them to a nearby hill called Ilicinus where she knew there was a fierce dragon and violent bulls which she hoped would dispose of these irritating visitors. The dragon, however, vanished in smoke at the sign of the Cross, and the bulls were reduced to quiet submission. They allowed themselves to be yoked to a cart and brought the body back to Lupa's Palace. The queen, disorientated by all these miracles, embraced Christianity and donated her palace as a burying ground for the apostle. Some say that

129 (opposite) *Main altar of the Parish Church of Santiago, Padrón, with beneath it the mooring post of the boat that brought the body of St James to Spain.*

two of the disciples remained with the Saint and were buried with him, while the rest went on preaching or returned to the Holy Land.

The legend resumes in the early ninth century, when in about 813 Bishop Theodemir of Iria Flavia, some few kilometres from Padrón, claimed to have found the tomb of St James through supernatural guidance. He cleared a wooded site, found the ruins of a building, a little courtyard with two graves, and a tiny chapel with a third grave. News travelled to all parts. King Alfonso II of Asturias came in haste, declared St James the protector of all Spain and built a modest church and a small monastery. Gifts accumulated; soon a settlement grew up around a site called by later generations Compostela. To complete the saga, at the Battle of Clavijo in the early stages of the Reconquest of Spain, the apostle appeared on a white horse in the sky above the Christian ranks and led them to victory over 70,000 Moors. As a gesture of gratitude, Ramiro I of Leon is said to have drawn up a document in 844 ordering that all Spain, conquered and to be conquered, should pay in perpetuity an annual offering made from the first fruits of the year's harvest and vintage, and handed over to the canons of the cathedral at Compostela. This is beyond doubt a forgery, because the Battle of Clavijo took place in 859. However, during the subsequent centuries these offerings, so-called *votos de Santiago*, were followed by innumerable donations from kings, nobles and clerics to make the bishop, later archbishop, one of the richest landowners in the Peninsula.

The case of St James and the accompanying legends in no way constitute a special case in medieval history. Where deep convictions are brought to play, proof comes easily to the promoter of a cause. But Christianity is very much concerned with the interlocking of the supernatural and the natural, and Christians feel an obligation to examine and understand the motives of their predecessors. The two propositions that St James preached in Spain and that his body was buried in Compostela have proved extremely improbable. In a fundamental study of 1900, Duchesne showed that up to 600 no one believed or proclaimed either of these assertions.[4] After this date a series of scattered references occur in various manuscripts. Finally, a martyrology of Usuard of St Germain des Prés, *c.* 865, mentions for the first time that St James was buried in Spain. Therefore the news follows the supposed uncovering of remains in a place called Compostela. The name Compostela itself, so long associated with popular legend and pictorial image of 'the star in the field' (*campus stellae*) or the Milky Way (*via lactea*) which pointed to the shrine, may in all probability refer to a graveyard, a little graveyard, from the Latin *compostum*, a burial-ground. So there may well have existed there an ancient cemetery. But why was it supposed to contain the body of St James, since no legends about his burial in Spain pre-date this discovery? The only local reference is a mention of the Saint on an inscribed stone of about 627 found during the 1940s in the Church of Santa María de Mérida. It could be that immigrants from the south in the eighth and ninth

130 (opposite) *Figure of St James (detail), Pórtico de la Gloria, Cathedral of Santiago de Compostela. This noble carving sits atop the trumeau or central column, to welcome the penitent. St James has traditionally been accorded a very special devotion by all of Christendom. He was the son of Zebedee, a fisherman of Galilee and Salome, and the brother of St John and St James the Lesser. He was called by the Master on the same day as St Peter and St Andrew, on the shores of Lake Galilee. Christ appointed him to teach the gospel, and he is believed to have preached in Spain. On his return to Jerusalem he was the first apostle to be martyred.*

131 *St James as a pilgrim, with staff, broad-brimmed hat, scallop and all-enveloping pilgrim cloak. This stone statue is in the museum at the Monastery of San Marcos in Leon, one of several museums devoted to St James along the pilgrim route.*

centuries brought their cults with them. One may further suppose that a local church was in need of some spiritual or social unity and chose a patron to give them that sense of coherence. Whatever the explanation, the choice of St James was a local affair and must be related to local conditions.

Apocryphal history may be contrived, like the supposed dating of the Battle of Clavijo, to trick out the gaps in a tale, but until the latter half of the ninth century there was no substantial interest in St James. The promoters of change were Alfonso III the Great of Asturias (866-910) and Sisnando, the Bishop of Iria Flavia (880-920). Alfonso was the first serious and generous benefactor of the Church of St James, and it may be that he was seeking a patron saint of another type to mould and preserve the Asturian kingdom. The historian R. A. Fletcher argues plausibly that Alfonso, with greater international awareness than his predecessors, sought to expand his patronage beyond the limits of Oviedo and push westwards to Galicia and south to the plains of Leon. There is a famous but suspect letter that gives substance to the king's intentions.[5] This letter, dated *c*.906, was written by Alfonso to the clergy of Tours and ostensibly deals with the purchase of an Imperial crown. But the king talks mainly of his reverence for St James, and for his relics and his miracles. The letter suggests that the tomb had already become a miracle-working object, possibly the centre of a local pilgrimage, and that Alfonso was keen to expand the cult.

Alfonso III had launched a movement which far outstripped his original intentions. He wanted a spiritual figure-head for his own 'imperial' plans, but instead his creation contributed to the fading of Oviedo and the Asturias into the background, since the seat of power moved south to Leon. Distinguished people began to visit the shrine; in 951 Bishop Gottschalk of Le Puy; in 961 the Archbishop of Rheims. But these were turbulent times. In 988 the Moors sacked Leon, and nine years later it was the turn of Santiago itself. The cathedral erected by Alfonso III was destroyed, although the relics were left untouched. With Leon thus weakened, the rising kingdom of Navarre became the dominant influence on the affairs of nearly all the Christian states of the north. There followed the creation of the kingdom of Castile, the linkage of Castile and Leon under one king, the reorganization of the spiritual life and the invitation of settlers, crusaders and pilgrims from France by a succession of monarchs, especially Alfonso VI of Castile and Leon. A contemporary of his in the latter half of the eleventh century was Diego Peláez, the Bishop of Compostela. It was he who thought of a magnificent cathedral of new design. Before he was deposed in 1088, Diego Peláez oversaw the construction of the east end up to the transepts. Work on this third great Compostela church was completed by two master-masons with French-sounding names, Bernard and Robert, under the eye of Santiago's first Archbishop, Diego Gelmírez (*c.* 1060-1140). He planned and built the nave of the church and also constructed the chapter buildings, the cloister and the

palace. He must have had an immense labour force at his disposal, including Moorish captives.

Compostela was not a quiet place during Diego's reign. His relations with the ambitious and expanding bourgeoisie involved major confrontations. The situation cannot be classified as a simple contest between a 'progressive bourgeoisie' and a 'reactionary episcopal seigneur' (according to Fletcher) since the Queen Urraca, Alfonso VII's boisterous mother, was an ambiguous element in a struggle in which the Archbishop at one point lost all power in the city and had his palace burned. The resentment had much to do with the nepotistic administration of the town, a continuing issue right up to the time of the Fonseca regime in the fifteenth and sixteenth centuries. It may be that the citizens objected to the flood of goods from outside and the presence of foreigners in authoritative positions. It is evident that Compostela, at the height of its popularity abroad in the early twelfth century, was not a tranquil centre of religious meditation.

The Bishop and the Queen in the palace heard the outbursts in the city and realized how much the traitors, the followers of Judas had inflamed the

132 *Carving of twin lions, Church of Notre Dame la Grande, Poitiers. The façade of this twelfth-century church is typical of later Poitevin churches, and is probably one of the best. The whole is richly and exuberantly carved and sculpted.*

inhabitants against them...How daring were the hands of evil! The perverse enemy set fire to the Basilica of St James. It began to burn from one side to the other, for much of it was covered in wood planks and woven straw...The flames reached up into the church of the Apostle and created everywhere a terrifying sight. Pilgrims from abroad who were visiting the shrine were bathed in tears. When the Bishop and the Queen saw that the plotters were ready to commit any crime, they realized they would not be safe in the palace and took refuge in the bell-tower...Then at last they began to attack the bell-tower where the Bishop and his men, the Queen and her following, had taken refuge... Realizing that these few could hold on, and that outcome was still unsure, the mob decide to burn them out. Protecting their heads with shields, they started a fire through one of the lower openings in the tower and heaped on everything that would burn.[6]

The queen was eventually allowed out and fled nearly naked, covered with mud and exhausted. The archbishop followed, disguised in a threadbare cape, slipping through holes torn in the upper storeys of adjacent timber houses until he reached a safe place, where he and a few friends escaped on horses provided by the Franks. This took place in 1117 and the same thing happened again in 1136, just four years before Diego's death on 6 April 1140.

Disturbed as they may have been by these savage outbursts, the pilgrims did not cease coming. Indeed their numbers increased, as did the international fame and the curative powers of the shrine. The visitors were of the highest standing: Archbishops of Mainz, Duke William X of Acquitaine, St Francis of Assisi, Louis VII of France, Henry the Lion, Duke of Saxony, Fernando and Isabel, the Catholic Monarchs, and Charles V, the Holy Roman Emperor, right down to Generalísimo Franco and Pope John Paul II in our own times. How-ever, from their number we must exclude Empress Matilda, who many writers had said made the pilgrimage after her husband Henry V died, bringing back the hand or forearm of St James which her father Henry I gave to Reading Abbey. No sources are ever quoted for the voyage, which almost certainly never occurred. The hand was indeed given by Henry; however, it came not from Santiago but from Torcello, near Venice.

To the figure of the Saint as pilgrim, of international reputation, became attached that of St James 'the Moorslayer', of specifically Peninsular interest. The 'Diploma of Ramiro I' was forged sometime after Diego's death in a period of financial difficulties and social strife in Compostela. One can understand how circumstances might have led to an attempt to harness St James's reputation to local needs. Just as Charlemagne and Roland were attached to the route itself, so St James was transformed into the proponent of what Spanish historians refer to as the *Reconquista* – the recovery of territory occupied by the Moors. There is not space here to join in the complicated debate over whether such a coherent policy ever existed in broad terms amongst the early Christian kingdoms. What does emerge from increasing

133 (opposite) *Seated figure of St James, main altar, Cathedral of Santiago de Compostela. The Baroque altar containing the Romanesque stone statue of St James dates from 1665 and was positioned so that pilgrims could stand behind and embrace the image.*

134 *Capital, chapter house, Cathedral of St Lazare, Autun. The cathedral is rich in sculpture, most of it by the hand of Gislebertus (twelfth century). His signature is on the tympanum.*

international research is that the association of St James with territorial gains along the frontier only gathered force in the late twelfth century, supported by papal declarations that military service in Spain was not distinct from that in the Holy Land. The Order of the Knights of St James, founded in that same period, was a response to those growing political aspirations. Such an interpretation of the apostle's role must be seen as a late and local accretion of the figure of the humble missionary martyr. This is not to deny that the special circumstances of the Peninsula were relevant to his fame. The advance of the Christian frontier to the south and the consequential diminishing population of the north encouraged immigration which was accompanied by a new spirituality and an ecclesiastical reform. The spiritual element should not be undervalued in this transformation of the north.

By the late twelfth century the route known variously as the *via jacobea*, *via lactea*, *via francigena*, *camino francés*, was well-established in northern Spain, while in the rest of Europe the ancillary routes and local places of devotion were adding their special identity to the many attractions of the principal shrine of Christendom. At this time Rome was still a mean city with no impressive new constructions; the route to the Holy Land was interrupted and restricted, and fraught with political disagreements. In the West, however, access to farthest Spain was open by land and sea, and the principalities did all they could to encourage visitors. A major shrine had just been built for the relics of the first martyred apostle whose powers to heal both body and soul were recognized by every senior ecclesiastic. A powerful spiritual movement had been launched in which the journey and its attendant difficulties was one of the indispensable experiences. Thousands, from all ranks of society, seized the chance.

The pilgrimage became one of the great mass religious manifestations in which the individual Christian, freed from the pressures of daily life, laboured to arrive at his destination in a spiritual state worthy to receive the benediction of the Saint. During the months of hazardous travel, the trivialities of secular life or the concerns of high office fell into perspective. The pilgrims were, and still are, afforded the opportunity to consider the ills of the flesh, the inevitability of death and the fearsome Day of Reckoning. These issues were emphasized and stressed at every stage of the journey with all the power available to the Church, its artists and craftsmen.

Today that power still resides in the surviving monuments and in the stones of the route. They do not talk with a negative voice. On the contrary, they speak of gain. However one values relics and their virtues, the benefits of voyaging with such a purpose are not yet exhausted. The twenty-third Psalm, which is in essence nomadic, spoke to Berceo when he composed the verses quoted in Chapter One. It also spoke to Kathleen Raine, the celebrated English religious poet, in the autumn of this present century:

I am that part that I must play,
I am the journey I must go,
All that I am I must endure
And bear the burden of my years
Of good and evil, time and place
Before the story all is told.
All that is possible must be
Before the concord can be full
Of earth's great cry of joy and woe.[7]

135 *Charity conquering Avarice, capital, chapter house, Cathedral of St Lazare, Autun. Many pilgrim churches carried instruction drawn from the Bible and from treatises on morals.*

136 *Torture of the damned, detail of tympanum (Fig. 28), Abbey Church of Ste Foy, Conques.*

† NOTES †

CHAPTER I

1 Gonzalo de Berceo, *Los milagros de Nuestra Señora*, ed. Brian Dutton (London, 1971), p. 29.

2 Walter Muir Whitehill, *Liber Sancti Jacobi*, 3 vols. (Compostela, 1944). Book Five has been edited separately, with a facing French translation by Jeanne Vielliard, *Le Guide du Pèlerin de Saint Jacques de Compostelle* (Macon, 1950, 1963).

3 Sumption, p. 125; *Liber Sancti Jacobi*, ed. cit., vol. 1, p. 155-7.

4 Ibid., p. 122.

5 Fletcher, p. 92.

6 Vázquez, vol. 1, p. 51.

7 Fletcher, p. 87.

8 Davies, p. 34.

9 A popular medieval manual of saints' lives and miracles written by Jacobus de Voragine (Jacopo de' Varazze, 1230-98), archbishop of Genoa. It was printed by Caxton at the end of the fifteenth century. See the *Golden Legend of Jacobus de Voragine*, translated and adapted from the Latin by Granger Ryan and Helmut Ripperger (New York, 1969), and R. Oursel, *Routes romanes: la route aux saints* (St Leger Vauban, 1982).

10 Mâle, pp. 282-315; Conant, 1966, pp. 91-106.

CHAPTER II

1 *Pilgrimage in old Rithme. Relations and Observations of Spaine in old English Rime* (c.1292) in Samuel Purchas, *Hakluytus Posthumus or Purchas His Pilgrimes*, vol. VII (Glasgow, 1905), p. 528.

2 Robert Southey, *Poetical Works*, vol. VII (London, 1857), p. 249. This legend is attributed to the Virgin and to Ste Foy and many other saints.

CHAPTER III

1 'Estonce era Castilla un pequenno rincón,
era de Castellanos Montes d'Oca mojón.' The narrative *Poema de Fernán González* about the first Count of Castile (920-70) was written *c*.1260 (?), possibly by a monk of the monastery of San Pedro de Arlanza, near Burgos.

2 Jiménez de Rada, *De rebus Hispaniae*, written *c*.1243.

3 Quoted and translated by Angus Mackay, *Spain in the Middle Ages: From Frontier to Empire, 1000-1500* (London, 1977), p. 52.

4 Domenico Laffi, *Viaggio in Ponente a San Giacomo di Galitia e Finisterrae* (Bologna, 1681), p. 184. First published 1673.

5 Suero de Quiñones, *Libro del passo honroso*, ed. A. Lebandeira Fernández (Madrid, 1977).

6 George Borrow, *The Bible in Spain* (London, 1843) ch. xxxii.

CHAPTER IV

1 There are two routes to Santiago from Villafranca. The majority went by Cebrero, but others chose to go by Lugo, turning to the right before Faba to Piedrafita, over the less arduous pass of Manzanal.

2 Controversy has never ceased over the design of the Cathedral. The French were first to claim its close affinity with St Sernin at Toulouse, but this was contested by the Spaniards who pointed out that Santiago had probably already been started in 1071 while the southern French Cathedral was not begun until 1080.

3 Padrón means 'stone marker'. The stone post to which the boat was supposedly moored can still be seen, in the shape of a Roman altar, under the main altar in the parish church of Padrón.

4 L. Duchesne, 'St-Jacques en Galice', *Annales du Midi*, 12 (1900) pp. 145-80.

5 Fletcher, Appendix C, pp. 317-23.

6 *Historia Compostellana*, chapter 114.

7 Kathleen Raine, 'In my seventieth year', *The Oracle in the Heart* (Dolmen Press, 1980).

† BIBLIOGRAPHY †

There have been many excellent works in different languages dealing with the road to the shrine of St James. As for those in English, some are records of individual efforts, others are scholarly investigations. Walter Starkie's *The Road to Santiago* (1951) and T. A. Layton's *The Way of Saint James* (1976) fall into the first category, while Horton and Marie-Hélène Davies's *Holy Days and Holidays: the Medieval Pilgrimage to Santiago* (1982) and R. A. Fletcher's *Saint James's Catapult: the Life and Times of Diego Gelmírez of Santiago de Compostela* (1984) are the latest of a long list of authoritative works. The most widely known study, which combines with elegance the personal memoir and assiduous reading in more than one language, is Edwin Mullins's *The Pilgrimage to Santiago* (1974). For those who seek a much wider and deeper knowledge of the medieval pilgrimage in general, Jonathan Sumption's *Pilgrimage: an Image of Medieval Religion* (1975) is indispensable.

Bottineau, T., *Les Chemins de St Jacques* (Paris, 1964).

Brown P., *The Cult of the Saints* (Chicago, 1981)

Collins, R., *Early Medieval Spain: Unity in Diversity, 400-1000* (London, 1983).

Conant, K. T., *The Early Architectural History of the Cathedral of Santiago de Compostela* (Cambridge, Mass., 1926).

Conant, K. T., *Carolingian and Romanesque Architecture, 800 to 1200* (Harmondsworth, 1966).

Cox, I. (ed.), *The Scallop: Studies of a Shell and Its Influences on Humankind* (London, 1957).

Davies, H. and M.-H., *Holy Days and Holidays: the Medieval Pilgrimage to Santiago* (London and Toronto, 1982).

Dupront, A., *Saint-Jacques de Compostelle: Puissances du pèlerinage* (Paris, 1985).

Fletcher, R. A., *Saint James's Catapult: the Life and Times of Diego Gelmírez of Santiago de Compostela* (Oxford, 1984).

Geary, P. J., *Furta Sacra: Thefts of Relics in the Central Middle Ages* (Princeton, 1978).

Goicoechea Arrondo, E., *Rutas Jacobeas* (Estella, 1971).

Harvey, J., *The Cathedrals of Spain* (London, 1957).

Hell, V. and H., *The Great Pilgrimages of the Middle Ages* (Tübingen, 1964; English trans. London, 1966).

Kendrick, T., *St James in Spain* (London, 1960).

King, G., *The Way of St James*, 3 vols. (New York, 1920).

Layton, T. A., *The Way of St James* (London, 1976).

Mâle, E., *Religious Art in France: the Twelfth Century: a Study of the Origins of Medieval Iconography* (Princeton, 1978).

Mullins, E., *The Pilgrimage to Santiago* (London, 1974).

Oursel, R., *Les Pelerins du moyen âge: les hommes, les chemins, les sanctuaires* (Paris, 1963).

Secret, J., *Saint Jacques et les chemins de Compostelle* (Paris, 1957).

Starkie, W., *The Road to Santiago* (London, 1951).

Stokstad, M., *Santiago de Compostela in the Age of the Great Pilgrimages* (Norman, 1978).

Stone, J. S., *The Cult of Santiago* (New York, 1927).

Sumption, J., *Pilgrimage: an Image of Medieval Religion* (London, 1975).

Valina Sampedro, E., *Guía del peregrino: el camino de Santiago* (Madrid, 1982).

Vázquez de Parga, L., Lacarra, J. M., Uría Ríu, J., *Las Peregrinaciones a Santiago de Compostela*, 3 vols. (Madrid, 1949; reprinted Oviedo, 1981).

Ward, B., *Miracles and the Medieval Mind: Theory, Record and Event, 1000-1215* (Philadelphia, 1982).

† INDEX †